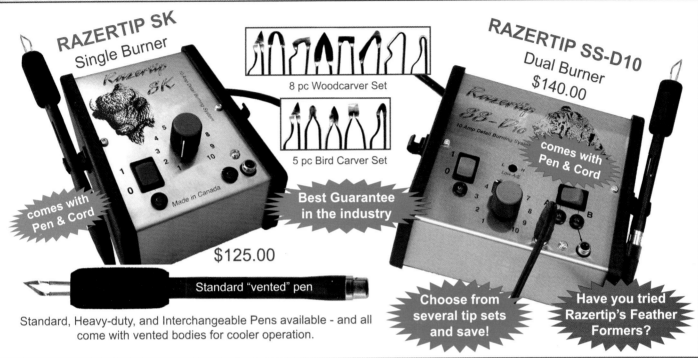

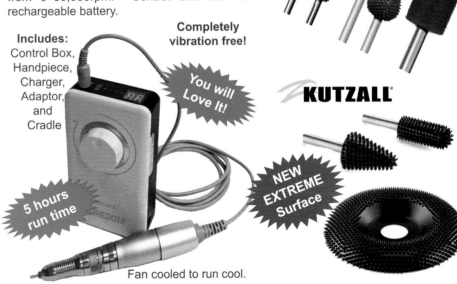

Wildfowl Carving
MAGAZINE
COMPETITION
2017
ANNUAL 2018

Contents

38

60

26

FROM THE EDITOR

MY FIRST COMPETITION

After years of looking at competitions from the outside as the editor of this fine publication, I got a change of perspective last year. WILDFOWL CARVING MAGAZINE, which I also edit, had run an article by Bob Lund and Gary Joe Bryan in its Winter 2017 issue about carving antique-style shorebird silhouettes. It looked like a fun project and I figured shorebirds would make excellent Christmas presents. I decided to carve some for my wife and another one for my parents.

For my wife, I decided to make a trio of a semipalmated plover, yellowlegs, and a golden plover. I found a great piece of weathered board at my sister's, plus some rusty old nails that would make ideal bills. I used one of the patterns from the magazine article and a couple from Del Herbert's Service Class Shorebirds workbench project. I followed the painting directions in the article, with some additional information from Del's book. For the eyes, I found a bag of golden rivets at a craft store. I think they are used to decorate jeans, but they looked like they would make perfect eyes.

I was right: making the shorebirds was a lot of fun. I was pleased with my efforts, crude as they were. The recipients seemed pleased, too.

And then I got the bright idea to enter my wife's birds into competition at the Ward World Championship. I entered them at the novice level in the bench class for shorebirds. There were some pretty ambitious entries there, and I was pretty sure I was going to get shut out. Every so often during the weekend I would leave the WILDFOWL CARVING MAGAZINE booth on the show floor and drift by the novice table to look at my birds and their competitors. At one point when I drifted past, I noticed that the judges had placed a yellow ribbon on my entry.

I had won third place in the shorebirds category. I couldn't stop grinning all day.

That was my first taste of competition. It was pretty exciting, even at my level. I can only guess at how intense it must be when you've devoted hundreds of hours working on a world-class piece and you're competing against the best wildfowl carvers in the world. I don't think I'll ever learn first-hand what that's like, but I'm satisfied with my experience.

In the following pages you are going to see just how good competitive wildfowl carving can get. I hope you'll be inspired by what you see—and maybe even enter a competition yourself if you haven't already. Believe me, it's worth it.

Tom Huntington

ON THE COVER: *Roy Barkhouse photographed Wayne Simkin's Canada goose at the Canadian National Wildfowl Carving Championship in March 2017. The goose won best in show and first in the Canadian Master Class.*

Editor
Tom Huntington

Graphic Designer
Brittnee Longnecker

Advertising Director
Jenny Latwesen

COMPETITION 2017,
A WILDFOWL CARVING MAGAZINE
publication, is published by AMPRY
PUBLISHING, LLC,
3400 Dundee Road, Suite 220,
Northbrook, IL 60062. Contents
copyright © 2018. All rights
reserved. Reproduction in whole
or in part without consent of the
publisher is prohibited.

Canadian GST #R137954772

Advertising: (847) 513-6095

All correspondence
should be addressed to:
Competition 2017
P.O. Box 490
New Cumberland, PA 17070
(847) 513-6057
Fax: (847) 513-6099

www.wildfowl-carving.com

ISBN: 978-1-945550-28-7

Printed in the U.S.A.

Want to add books like these to your shelf?

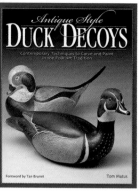 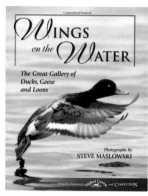   

Join the *Wildfowl Carving* Book Club! It's easy as 1-2-3!

1 Join the *Wildfowl Carving* Book Club and receive our latest release hot off the press! Becoming a member is 100% FREE, and you can cancel your membership at any time.
Call us toll-free to join the book club at (877) 762 - 8034
Canadian customers call (866) 375 - 7257
Give PROMO Code: **WFBCC17**
Or join the book club online at www.WildfowlCarvingMagazineService.com/bookclub

2 After we process your membership, we will send you our latest book.

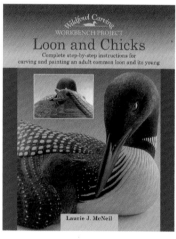

Pssst!

We typically release two new books each year. Our Book Club is the best way to guarantee your copies at an incredible discount!

3 Love the book?
Just pay the discounted price + S&H
Not loving the book?
No problem! Return the book at our expense

WFBCC17

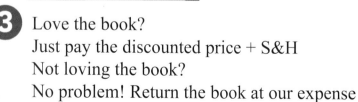
Become A Member Of The Book Club Today!

CORE SOUND DECOY FESTIVAL

December 3 – 4, 2016: Harkers Island, North Carolina

Text by Stan Rule

Photography by Brent Hood

Belted Kingfisher by Walter Gaskill. Best of Show,
IWCA Decorative Miniature, Open.

Scaup Hen by Walter Gaskill. Best of Show, IWCA-style Decoy, Open.

Each year, the Core Sound Decoy Festival and its community bond over an appreciation for the art of decoy carving. That culturally rich heritage and the legacy of the region's waterfowl hunters provide the core of the Core Sound Decoy Carvers Guild, which hosts the festival on the first full weekend each December at the Harkers Island Elementary School. Thanks to hard work by dedicated volunteers, the festival continues to be a popular and successful event. The 29th annual festival proved to be one of the largest yet, attracting hundreds of attendees, competitors, and exhibitors.

The featured carver for the 2016 festival was Robbie Robertson of Greensboro, North Carolina. Robbie's style has graced more than 3,000 decoys. He usually carves contemporary gunners but also enjoys creating "antique" shorebirds. Robbie's birds are striking, but people value him even more for his personality and energy.

Competition was strong at the 2016 show, with nearly 400 entries across the various divisions, including the 2016 International Waterfowl Carvers Association Working Decoy Championship. (Those winners appeared in last year's COMPETITION.) The local flavor included Core Sound-style, root head, and contemporary antique divisions along with the youth competition on Sunday's Youth Day.

Visitors could purchase items from a hundred decoy- and hunting-related vendors from nine states, and visit artifact exhibits by guild members. In addition, the Carolina Decoy Collectors Association had an extensive presentation. Other opportunities included carving demonstrations, a head-whittling contest, a live auction of antique decoys, children's decoy painting, retriever demonstrations, the N.C. Wildlife Commission's Safari Exhibit, a small duck impoundment, and—when hunger struck—local seafood and trimmings. Shuttles were available to reach the Core Sound Waterfowl Museum to see the Waterfowl Weekend events and exhibits there.

The festival helps support guild activities through the year, including youth camp scholarships, a successful kids' carving program, support of various community needs, and educational programs for members and guests. It also serves as a fundraiser for the school. This community volunteer effort translates into year-round community benefits.

The 2017 festival took place in December. You can find more information on the guild's website, *https://decoyguild.com*, and on its Facebook page.

Eurasian Wigeon Drake by Walter Gaskill. Best of Show, IWCA-style Decoy, Open.

Black-bellied Plover by Walter Gaskill. Best of Show, IWCA Gunning Shorebird Decoy, Open.

King Eider Drake by Jon Jones. Third Best of Show, IWCA-style Decoy, Open.

Red Phalarope by Gary Joe Bryan. Second Best of Show, IWCA Gunning Shorebird Decoy, Open.

Sora Rail by Walter Gaskill. Third Best of Show, IWCA Gunning Shorebird Decoy, Open.

Wood Duck Drake by Fred Miller. Best of Show, IWCA Decorative Life-size Floating Decoy, Open.

Red-billed Teal by Craig Mortimer. Second Best of Show, IWCA Decorative Life-size Floating Decoy, Open.

Bufflehead Drake by Warren Brown. Third Best of Show, IWCA Decorative Life-size Floating Decoy, Open.

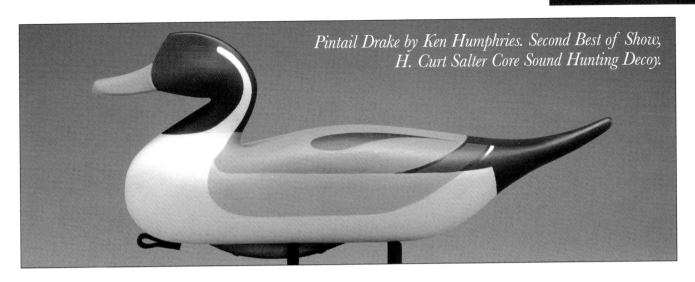

Pintail Drake by Ken Humphries. Second Best of Show, H. Curt Salter Core Sound Hunting Decoy.

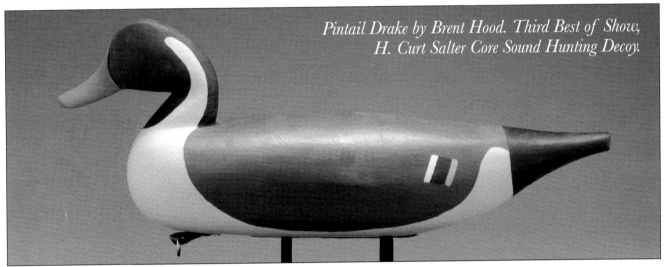

Pintail Drake by Brent Hood. Third Best of Show, H. Curt Salter Core Sound Hunting Decoy.

Wood Duck Drake by Robin Oliver. Best of Show, IWCA Canvas Decoy.

American Kestrel by Karen Hess. Best of Show, IWCA Decorative Life-size Non-floating, Open.

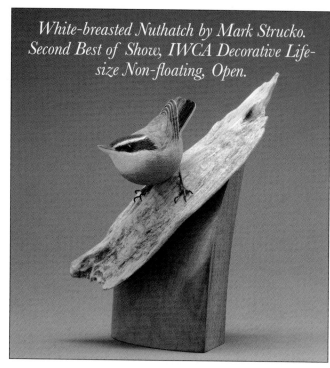

White-breasted Nuthatch by Mark Strucko. Second Best of Show, IWCA Decorative Life-size Non-floating, Open.

American Kestrel by Mark Strucko. Third Best of Show, IWCA Decorative Life-size Non-floating, Open.

American Kestrel by Randy Hansen. Best of Show, IWCA Decorative Life-size Non-floating, Intermediate.

Shorebird by Ken Humphries. Best of Show, Root Head Decoy.

Brant by Ken Humphries. Third Best of Show, Contemporary Antique Decoy.

Ruddy Duck Drake by Marty Linton. Best of Show, Contemporary Antique Decoy.

Red-breasted Merganser Drake by Ben Heinemann.
Second Best of Show, Contemporary Antique Decoy.

Tickled by his strong showing in the 2016 Core Sound Decoy Festival carving competitions, Ken Humphries said he felt like "grinning all week." Success in the Core Sound-style, contemporary antique, and root head divisions demonstrated his emerging proficiency. Ken describes himself as being "full-bore" into carving following a circuitous path that now sees him balancing carving time with work, coaching youth baseball, and leading scouts. He still finds time to mentor son Sam in his own decoy making.

As he was completing his degree in commercial art and graphic design, Ken became interested in local boatbuilding in Marshallberg, North Carolina, in Carteret County, and ended up following that path instead. Although a native of Pamlico County, Ken now calls Marshallberg "the right spot for us." He carved his first decoy with a grinder at the boatyard in 1998 and left it unpainted to give to a friend. He next did a rig of blackheads before turning his attention to flat art with oils. He pursued this successfully—even full time—for three years. About three years ago, he reached another turning point when he was doing a rendering of a vintage Eldon and Roy Willis decoy. The painting reignited his interest in creating decoys. Asked by a Ducks Unlimited chapter to create an art piece for a benefit auction, he decided to do a decoy instead. It generated some strong bidding and recharged his creative energy.

Preferring traditional hand tools and working from his own drawings as patterns, Ken emphasizes form that shows "flow coming together" in the carving, coupled with painting lines that "match up" in a pattern that pleases the eye. He describes the combination as "sexy." Being adamant about proportions, he follows the "rule of thirds." As an example, Ken refers to a brant by Portsmouth's George O'Neal. It has a long sweeping tail, a feeder neck and head, and pleasant lines of body and rump. Each section has its own pleasing features. Ken often likes to accentuate one feature to catch the eye even more. He finishes off with thinned spar varnish, light sanding, and oil paints, often house paints mixed to his liking. The decoys get no additional finish, but he might rub them down with cardboard to dull the paint a little. He does a variety of carvings, from battery decoys to refined birds. He will recycle elements in each but, at the same time, continue the process of defining his own style.

One thing is clear: Ken Humphries has become part of the rich heritage created by North Carolina's Marshallberg and Downeast carvers.

Scaup Drake by Ken Humphries. Best of Show, H. Curt Salter Core Sound Hunting Decoy.

STAN RULE

CALIFORNIA OPEN WILDLIFE ARTS FESTIVAL

February 18 – 19, 2017: San Diego, California

Text by Del Herbert

Photography by Carter Rote

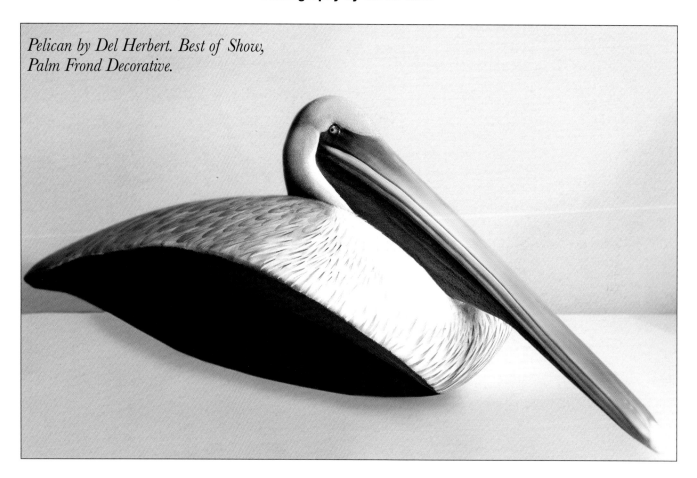

Pelican by Del Herbert. Best of Show, Palm Frond Decorative.

It is with a heavy heart that I write about the 44th and last California Open Wildlife Arts Festival. The show had been getting smaller over the past several years. Of course, there was a cadre of loyal supporters, but the show had experienced difficulty attracting new and energetic people. Cost increased while participation and attendance dropped. Pacific Southwest Wildlife Arts remains a viable club, but it was unable to sustain the high standards and quality that had been the hallmark of the California Open over the years.

The final California Open show kicked off on February 17 with a cocktail party and buffet dinner for the carvers, exhibitors, and their guests. After voting for the people's choices for cocktail carvings and postcard art paintings, the attendees had a chance to bid on this wonderful art and add it to their collections. Old and new friends shared their favorite stories to start the weekend.

On to the show. At the California Open this year, 97 artists entered 157 pieces in the competition. While this was a decline in numbers, everyone agreed that the quality of the entries was outstanding. Judging of the floating entries took place in the 50' x 50' fountain outside the showroom. This venue proved popular with both the carvers and the general public.

Introduced by Bob Sutton in the early 1990s, the palm frond competition went on to become a signature event for the California Open. Thanks to the support of Doug and Ellen Miller, this category has grown tremendously over the years. As you can see in the following photos, 2017 continued the tradition. The palm frond category has even been adopted by the Ward World Championship, the Pacific Flyway Decoy Association show in Sacramento, and the Ohio Decoy Collectors and Carvers Association, so its rich heritage will continue.

Daniel Montano again sponsored the youth painting event. This year the subject was a feather on canvas, and 25 young artists took home their artistic interpretations. Hopefully, these youngsters will retain interest in wildfowl art for years to come.

Again, it is with a sense of sadness that I report that this was the final California Open Wildlife Arts Festival. Hopefully, the other shows around North America will continue to prosper as they perpetuate this truly American art form.

Hoopoe by R.D. Wilson. Second Best of Show, Palm Frond Decorative.

Toucan by Mike Dowell. Third Best of Show, Palm Frond Decorative.

Shoveler by John Gewerth. Best of Show, Palm Frond Decoy.

Grebe by Del Herbert. Second Best of Show, Palm Frond Decoy.

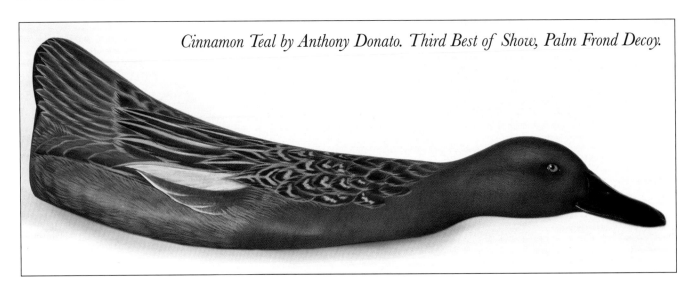

Cinnamon Teal by Anthony Donato. Third Best of Show, Palm Frond Decoy.

Merganser Drake by Tom Christie. Second Best of Show, IWCA-style Decoy, Open.

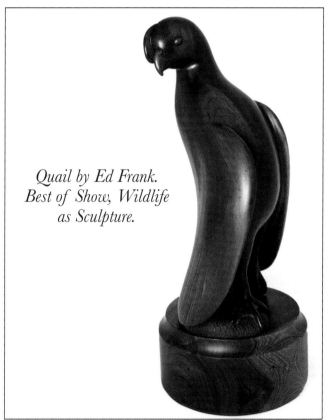

Quail by Ed Frank. Best of Show, Wildlife as Sculpture.

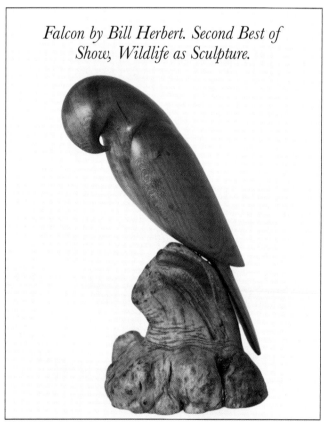

Falcon by Bill Herbert. Second Best of Show, Wildlife as Sculpture.

Green-winged Teal Drake by Leonard Rousseau.
Second Best of Show, Decorative Life-size Floating, Open.

Shoveler Hen by Anthony Donato. Best of Show,
Decorative Life-size Floating, Open.

"I usually go into a show expecting to get my butt kicked," says veterinary surgeon Steven Cogar. "I don't ever go into a show expecting to win. Doing that takes all the fun out of the competitions." When he likes a bird enough to enter it in competition, he's still happy with it no matter how it does.

Cogar's work has been foiling his expectations lately, though, and he earned top spots in the IWCA working decoy championship at Core Sound in 2016, and in 2017 at both the ODCCA and the California Open.

Cogar began as an "avid" waterfowl hunter who wanted to hunt over his own decoys. He carved his first bird in 2007, took a long break during his internship and residency, and picked it up again around 2012 after moving to North Carolina and "lucking in" to a group of carvers that included Walter "Brother" Gaskill, Jack Cox, and Patrick Eubanks—"Yeah. No-namers for sure, huh?" Cogar says. So far, he has carved about 200 decoys and maybe a half-dozen style birds.

Cogar credits Gaskill with inspiring him to build his own private aviary, now home to "just about every species" of North American puddle ducks and divers. The aviary has been "a huge game-changer" in the overall quality of his work, he says. Cogar draws his patterns from reference photos on the Internet but comes back to the aviary for details. "You really can't replace having the bird in hand when it comes to getting accuracy of color or feather layout." Occasionally he will float his latest decoy carving in his duck pond to gauge how it looks next to the real thing.

Cogar has a background in black-and-white drawing, but painting remains a challenge. "Someone can show you how to carve, and it can be broken down into sequential steps that can be reproduced. With painting, what one person shows you is going to be nearly impossible for you to reproduce, even with the same brushes and paints. It's really trial and error. You can't replace time behind the paintbrush. That's the only way you get good at painting."

His favorite bird? The northern shoveler. "To me it's one of the more gorgeous birds we have as far as coloration and details. It has that spoon-shaped bill, it has a nice iridescent green head, the coloration of the side pockets is sort of a rust color, and white markings on the back make it stand out."

Favorite project? The fully carved rocking horse he's started for his infant daughter. So far, he's invested some 300 hours—"My goal for that is her first birthday."

Goldeneye Drake by Steven Cogar. Second Best of Show, IWCA-style Decoy, Amateur.

Ringneck Hen by Steven Cogar. Best of Show, IWCA-style Decoy, Amateur.

Hooded Merganser Drake by Bunny Farley. Best of Show, Decorative Life-size Non-floating, Open.

Short-eared Owl by Haruhio Sakakura. Second Best of Show, Decorative Life-size Non-floating, Open.

Golden Plover by Gary De Cew. Best of Show, Decorative Miniature, Open.

Scaup Hen by Leonard Rousseau. Second Best of Show, Decorative Miniature, Open.

Godwit by R.D. Wilson. Best of Show, Soon-to-be-Antiques, Pristine.

Reddish Egret by Del Herbert. Best of Show, Decorative Smoothie Waders.

Lapwing by Gary Joe Bryan. Best of Show, IWCA-style Shorebirds, Open.

Canvasback by R.D. Wilson. Second Best of Show, Soon-to-be-Antiques, Worn.

Pintail by R.D. Wilson. Best of Show, Soon-to-be-Antiques, Worn.

Pintail by R.D. Wilson. Second Best of Show, Soon-to-be-Antiques, Pristine.

OHIO DECOY COLLECTORS AND CARVERS ASSOCIATION

March 11 – 12, 2017: Strongsville, Ohio

Text by Bob Lund

Photography by Bruce Richert

The 40th annual Ohio Decoy Collectors and Carvers show and sale, featuring 20 waterfowl and fish carving competitions, brought a record crowd of enthusiastic followers to the Holiday Inn in Strongsville. Highlights included a tribute in honor of world champion carver Sonny Bashore, known for his artistic hunting-style duck and fish decoys and duck calls. Another highlight was the presentation of *The Million Dollar Duck* documentary, which aired on the Animal Planet

Green-winged Teal Hen by Pat Godin.
Best of Show, IWCA-style Decoy, Open.

channel and featured six artists who competed in the Federal duck stamp competition. Two of them, Adam Grimm and Tim Taylor, were on hand at the show throughout the weekend.

Much of the show took place in the hotel ballroom, but there was also plenty of activity for the pool contest, one of largest in the country. Many spectators at the pool sought out the decoy makers and made offers to buy decoys to hunt over, an indication of the high quality of work in this year's competition.

Tom Christie presented an excellent seminar on painting while Willy McDonald and Brian Ballard followed tradition by demonsrating their carving and painting techniques throughout the weekend. The Run-a-muck group again carved a six-bird rig for the pool contest and worked with a Wounded Warrior to share their skills at decoy making.

Pat Godin swept the IWCA-style decoy contest by winning the top three best of shows with a green-winged teal hen, a pintail, and a king eider. In the IWCA floating decorative decoy contest, Anthony Donato took top honors with a shoveler, and Pat took second and third best of shows with a wigeon and a wood duck.

Bruce DiVaccaro won first and second in the IWCA shorebird championship contest with an upland sandpiper and a Hudsonian godwit. A marbled godwit by Todd Van Wieren took third.

Best of show for decorative fish carving went to Sonny Bashore and his trout on mushrooms plaque. John Snow won second and third with a brown trout plaque and a crappie plaque. Sonny also took best of show with an outstanding jig stick, with second and third going to Ronnie Mapes and Wayne Baldwin. John Snow won the fish decoy best of show with a cutthroat trout, while Maurice Stiff took second and third with a yellow perch and fire tiger.

Two swans painted by artist Tim Taylor that were featured in *The Million Dollar Duck* won the flat art contest. His stunning painting will be featured on the 2018 show button. Keren Sung became Ohio's Federal junior duck stamp winner with a colored pencil drawing of green-winged teal.

The 41st annual ODCCA show will take place March 9–11, 2018, once again at the Holiday Inn in Strongsville. The show schedule and hotel information are available *www.odcca.net*. Vendors can call Wayne Baldwin at (419) 674-4361 for details about tables in the ballroom or a first-floor room. You can also find information on the ODCCA Facebook page.

Wigeon Drake by Pat Godin. Second Best of Show, Decorative Life-size Floating. Open. (Anthony Donato's best of show winner is on page 20.)

King Eider Drake by Pat Godin. Third Best of Show, IWCA-style Decoy, Open.

Pintail Hen by Pat Godin. Second Best of Show, IWCA-style Decoy, Open.

Wood Duck Drake by Pat Godin. Third Best of Show, Decorative Life-size Floating. Open.

Canada Goose by Vincent Ciola. Best of Show, IWCA-style Decoy, Amateur.

Pintail Drake by Gary Doviak. Best of Show, Cocktail Bird.

Redhead Drake by Ryan Steed. Best of Show, Decorative Life-size Floating. Intermediate

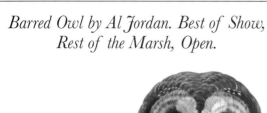

Barred Owl by Al Jordan. Best of Show, Rest of the Marsh, Open.

Pygmy Owl by Al Jordan. Second Best of Show, Rest of the Marsh, Open.

Magpie by Al Jordan. Third Best of Show, Rest of the Marsh, Open.

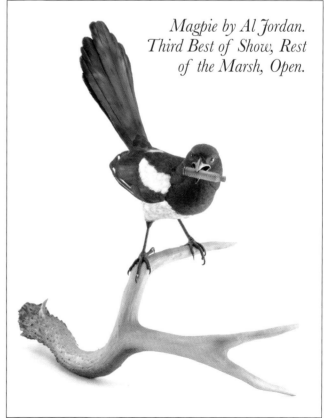

Juan Kingfisher by Gary McNeely. Second Best of Show, Rest of the Marsh, Miniatures, Open.

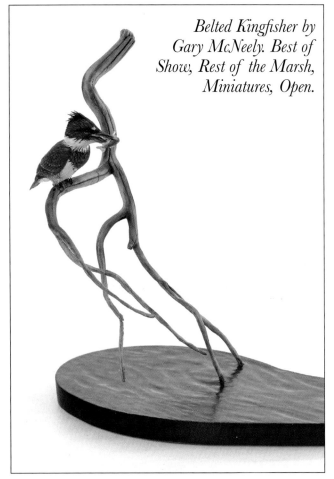

Belted Kingfisher by Gary McNeely. Best of Show, Rest of the Marsh, Miniatures, Open.

Pheasant by Sandy Czajka. Third Best of Show, Rest of the Marsh, Miniatures, Open.

Text by Sandy Oravec

Brad Falkinburg was a college intern in wetlands management at Ohio's Winous Point Shooting Club, the oldest continuously operating duck hunting club in North America, when he read an article in Ducks Unlimited about carving wooden decoys. "And I thought, 'Boy, that sounds like fun,'" he recalls. Someone suggested cork would be easier to carve, and Brad set out to make a rig of 36 blue-winged teal decoys. "I had to buy this giant chunk of cork, so I decided I was going to make as many decoys as I possibly could out of it." He still hunts over them today.

The project taught Brad something about himself: he paints fast. "I probably go too fast," he admits. It was the challenge of carving and painting a bird from start to finish at a show that got Brad hooked on entering competitions. He's done well in live carving and painting events, and this year he took best of show at the ODCCA event where you carve and prime at home, and paint at the show.

Brad prepares for those live events. "I do bring a lot of reference material to the show," he says. "Sometimes I'll even carve and paint a decoy of the same bird before the show as practice." At the show, he'll map out feather groups with a watercolor pencil, then apply the feathers themselves with stencils and airbrush, and finally finish with a detail brush.

You'll see the Falkinburg name more than once in the 2017 ODCCA winners' lists. Brad always does a cocktail bird (he took third in 2017), and he always does a dove (second best of show). The other Falkinburg names you'll see are his father, Herb (who caught the carving bug from his son; his goose took third place in "It Ain't Vintage Yet" for confidence), and his son, Ethan, who placed first in the youth silhouette contest, and his brother, Matt, longtime ODCCA contest chairman and supporter.

Brad works as an ecologist, goes duck hunting as often as he can, and creates most of his decoys during the winter months, usually after the family is in bed. He carves almost exclusively on commission—decoys and decoy urns for hunting dogs—and also responds to some unexpected requests. When 2016 Ward Living Legend Del Herbert saw Brad's 2008 ODCCA cocktail bird—a lesser yellowlegs that looked as if it had been stuffed into a glass—he requested one exactly like it. "World champion shorebird carver comes to me. Made my day," Brad says. Recently, he created decoys of the endangered Hawaiian stilt for scientists seeking to attract and band the shorebird. One of the scientists sent a video showing a stilt challenging one of Brad's decoys. That, Brad says, "was really cool."

You can see Brad's work at his website, *http://falkinburg-decoys.weebly.com*.

Turkey by Brad Falkinburg. Third Best of Show, Cocktail Bird.

Red-necked Phalarope by Andy Chlupsa. Second Best of Show, IWCA-style Shorebird, Open. (See Bruce DiVaccaro's best of show winner on page 99.)

Wood Duck Hen by Glen Sweet. Best of Show, Ladies Day in the Pool.

Goldeneye by Ken Stuparyk. Best of Show, Wildfowlers Single Decoy.

Hooded Merganser by Ken Ault. Best Hooded Merganser. Third Best of Show, Wildfowlers.

Goldeneyes by Gary Hanson. Best of Show, Wildfowlers Shooting Rig.

Canada Goose by Ken Hussey. Best of show, "It Ain't Vintage Yet." (You can see Ken's second best of show winner on page 45.)

Goldeneye by Scott Green. Third Best of show, "It Ain't Vintage Yet."

Curlew by Gary Joe Bryan. Second Best of Show, Working Shorebird Decoy. (Bruce DiVaccaro's best of show winner is on page 99.)

YOUR FREE TRIAL OF

Wildfowl Carving MAGAZINE

Join the premium community for carvers! Claim your FREE, no-risk issue of *Wildfowl Carving* Magazine.

- Sign up to receive your 100% FREE trial issue.

- Love the magazine? Simply pay the invoice for one full year (3 more issues for a total of 4).

- Don't love the magazine? No problem! Keep the free issue as our special gift to you, and you owe absolutely nothing!

Free, No-Risk Issue!

Claim Your FREE Trial Issue Today!
Call us toll-free for your free issue at (877) 762 – 8034
Canadian customers call (866) 375 – 7257
Use PROMO Code: WFC172

- -

Discover Inspiration, Techniques & Tutorials in Every Issue!

Yes! Rush my FREE issue of *Wildfowl Carving* Magazine and enter my subscription. If I love it, I'll simply pay the invoice for $37.95* for a one year subscription (3 more issues for a total of 4). In the unlikely event that I'm not satisfied, I'll return the invoice marked "cancel" and owe absolutely nothing.

SEND NO MONEY NOW – WE'LL BILL YOU LATER!

Cut out (or copy) this special coupon and mail to:
Wildfowl Carving Magazine Subscription Department
PO Box 2263
Williamsport, PA 17703-2263

First Name	Last Name

Postal Address

City	State/Province	Zip/Postal Code

Email Address

*Canadian subscribers add $4/year for S&H + taxes. Please allow 6-8 weeks for delivery of the first issue.

WFC172

CANADIAN NATIONAL WILDFOWL CARVING CHAMPIONSHIP

March 17 – 18, 2017: Waterloo, Ontario

Text by Peter McLaren

Photography by Roy Barkhouse

The weather during the 2017 Canadian National Wildfowl Carving Championship was quite cool with little sun, but no snow. The competition itself was anything but cool, with 112 carvers entering 201 birds in what was a revamped setting for the show at the Manulife Financial Sportsplex in Waterloo. This was the show's 28th annual outing, and it saw the introduction of a new competition class, the "Canadian Master." Carvers competing to win Canadian Master must have won one best of class or three first-place ribbons in the open class. Fifteen carvers entered 25 birds in this new class, and Pat Godin, Dave Ricci, Bruce Lepper, Jim Van Oosten, and

Canada Goose by Wayne Simkin. Best of Show and First, Canadian Master Class. (Pat Godin's second best of show winner for Canadian Master Class is on page 28.)

Wayne Simkin each won firsts in this inaugural event. Wayne took best of class, with Pat Godin second and Jason third. This order of finish was repeated in the best of show competition.

The open class attracted 27 carvers and 51 birds. Alex Rios Fernandez from Puerto Rico took best of class, with Quebec's Joe Tamborra taking second and Jim Edsall of Nova Scotia third. Laurie Snelling won best of class at the intermediate level, with Robin Deruchie and Debra Durfy taking second and third. Terry Wilson won best of class for novices, followed by Morgan Walker, who took both second and third. Daryl Chevalier was tops in beginners; Sierra Eskritt was second and Brian Wooding third.

The purchase awards are always hotly contested, and this year was no exception. The M & T Printing Group once again sponsored a purchase award, this year for a life-size male burrowing owl. The prize value was $3,500 (Canadian). Bruce Lepper took first, George Mechelse won second, and Laurie Truehart was third. Ontario Tool and Die Company's purchase award ($3,000) was for a pair of golden-crowned kinglets. Bruce Lepper won this one, too, with Jim Edsall coming in second and Martin Ward taking third. Dan and Patricia Meloche sponsored a purchase award ($1,200) for a miniature male blue jay. Greg Gillespie's jay came out the winner, with Tom Baldwin taking second and Winston Smith third. Rubberline Products Ltd.'s purchase award had a value of $800 and was for a pair of champagne waterfowl. Jason Lucio's won, with Gilles Prud'homme and Bob Lavender coming in second and third.

The members of the Grand Valley Woodcarvers are to be thanked for all the work they did to prepare for and carry out the show. Besides producing a stellar event, club members picked up 27 ribbons, including a best of class in novice. The 29th annual show will take place in March 2018. Visit www.canadiannationals.net *www.canadiannationals.net* for dates and information.

Torrent Duck Drake by Jason Lucio. Third Best of Show, Third, Canadian Master Class.

Prairie Warbler by Alex Rios Fernandez. First Best of Class, Open.

Surf Scoter Drake by Joe Tamborra. Second Best of Class, Open.

Blue Jay by Greg Gillespie. First, Dan and Patricia Meloche Purchase Award.

Screech Owl by Laurie Snelling. First Best of Class, Intermediate.

Burrowing Owl by Bruce Lepper. First, M&T Printing Group Purchase Award.

Canvasbacks by Jason Lucio. First, Rubberline Products, Ltd., Champagne Ducks Purchase Award.

Golden-crowned Kinglets by Bruce Lepper. First, Ontario Tool and Die Company Purchase Award.

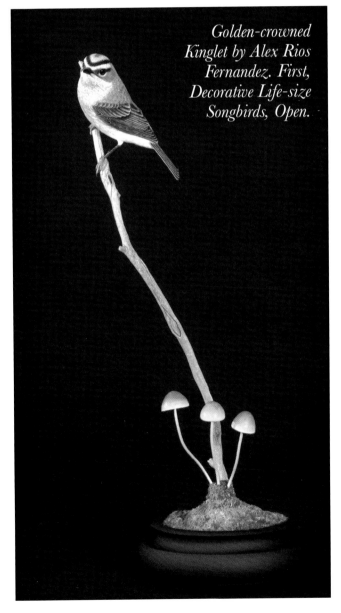

Golden-crowned Kinglet by Alex Rios Fernandez. First, Decorative Life-size Songbirds, Open.

Linda and Zenon Gawel

Text by Deborah Sandilands

Linda and Zenon Gawel are a creative carving couple. Zenon has carved for more than two decades. Linda was a flat artist who has been interested in color since she was a child when Zenon introduced her to carving about ten years ago. He has guided her and inspired her to do better and better. At the 2017 Ward World Championship, Linda won first-place ribbons at the novice level for her merlin, lesser scaup, and bufflehead, and second for her quail and chipping sparrow. Zenon won a second in intermediate for his lesser scaup.

Both Gawels use acrylic paints which they layer on to build up the color. Zenon will carve anything, and has even made decoys out of old telephone poles. Linda likes carving ducks and shorebirds and prefers tupelo or basswood. Recently, Zenon's brother cut them 10 four-foot basswood logs, and Linda and Zenon left them in the garage to air dry. One day their sons dropped by, spotted the logs, and decided they'd help their dad by cutting the wood up for the fireplace!

Zenon and Linda are grateful to have art they both love and understand and can communicate about. They even share the ability to critique each other's work without arguing. They have passed their love of carving to their grandchildren, who like to visit the carving room and work with the power tools their grandparents have taught them to use. Perhaps we will see carvings from the Gawel family well into the future.

They both have taken on the challenge of teaching members of the Grand Valley Woodcarvers how to carve and paint a killdeer. In addition, Zenon has established himself as an ambassador for the Canadian National Wildfowl Carving Championship every March and has co-chaired the show for many years. The carving world is lucky to have such generous promoters of the art form.

Lesser Scaup Drake by Linda Gawel.

Hooded Merganser Drake by Ray Tourangeau. First, Decorative Miniature Wildfowl, Open.

Gyrfalcon by Winston Smith. First, Decorative Birds of Prey, Open.

American Woodcock by William Berge. First, Decorative Birds of Prey, Open.

Vermilion Flycatcher by Bruce Lepper. First, Canadian Master Class Life-size Songbirds with Habitat.

Broad-winged Hawk by Jim Van Oosten. First, Canadian Master Class Birds of Prey and Upland Game Birds with Habitat.

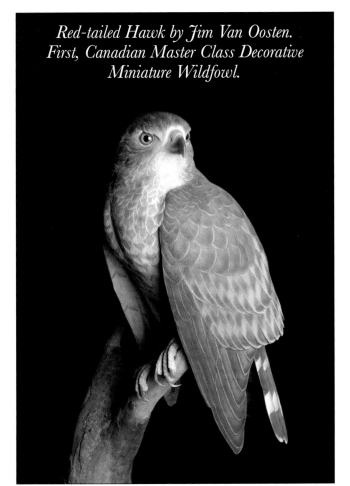

Red-tailed Hawk by Jim Van Oosten. First, Canadian Master Class Decorative Miniature Wildfowl.

Common Cinnamon Teal by Bruce Mifflin. First, Decorative Life-size Floating Ducks, Open.

Hooded Merganser Hen by Dave Ricci. First, Canadian Master Class Working Decoys.

Eider by Ken Hussey. First, Contemporary Decoy Class.

PACIFIC BRANT CARVING AND ART SHOW

April 8 – 9, 2017: Parksville, British Columbia

Text by Bill Beese

Photography by Dennis Drechsler

Yellow-shafted Flicker by Bob Lavender. Best of Show, Wildlife, Expert.

The Vancouver Island Woodcarvers organized its 27th annual woodcarving competition as part of the month-long Brant Wildlife Festival. The festival celebrates the return of brant geese to the eastern shores of Vancouver Island near the communities of Parksville and Qualicum Beach. Thousands of birds stop there to feast on eelgrass and herring eggs before continuing their journeys to Alaska. Coordinated by the Nature Trust of British Columbia, the 2017 festival included nature talks, tours, a birding competition, and other family events.

The Pacific Brant show has grown to be one of Canada's best-known woodcarving competitions, and many prairie carvers migrate west to "The Brant" each spring to escape the last bite of winter. One of the show's goals is to raise environmental awareness by showcasing artwork inspired by wildfowl, fish, and other wildlife. Although those subjects provide the focus, the competition also includes woodturning and other carving categories, as well as commercial booths featuring the region's top wildlife artists, photographers, and sculptors.

This year's competition attracted 109 carvers, 304 entries, and more than 800 visitors—an increase in carvings and visitors over last year. Winners took home $2,500 in cash, plus rosettes, medallions, and trophies across five skill levels. Best of show winners were Bob Lavender (expert), Robert Gander (advanced), Jim Price (intermediate), Wayne MacDonald (novice), Sophia Labonte (youth 11 and under), Dyson Blitterswyk (youth 12–14), and Lin Zhuolin Wu (youth 15–18). The endangered species competition, featuring the burrowing owl, was won by Sharon Hubbard (expert), Randy Joy (advanced) and Wayne MacDonald (novice). Entries in the popular "cocktail" class were auctioned after the competition; the three winners were Bob Lavender (air), Diane Craven (water), and Malcolm Ho-You (land). Three special "best of species" awards, sponsored by Cabela's Canada, went to Malcolm Ho-You (green-winged teal drake), Jack Tucker (spruce grouse), and

Barry Saunders (least sandpiper). Winners of the live head-painting competition were Bob Lavender (first), Bill Beese (second), and Harold Last (third).

The judging panel included World Champion Lynn Branson, plus other expert carvers and local naturalists. A dozen carvers enjoyed a two-day seminar on airbrushing a blue jay with Bob Lavender. Cam Merkle generously contributed his auctioneering skills and demonstrated Razertip Feather Former™ woodburning tips. The show also featured a youth painting workshop. Participants took home a brant silhouette and ribbons. Carvers and guests enjoyed a wildlife photography seminar by Alan Cornall, shopped at Island Woodcraft and carving sales tables, bid on live and silent auction items, and watched carving and woodturning demonstrations. Many carvers attended the Brant Festival's "Celebrate Nature" dinner on Saturday evening. And just two blocks from the show, you could walk the sandy beach and see flocks of feeding brant.

The 2018 carving competition will be held April 7–8 in beautiful British Columbia. You can visit the show website (*www.thebrant.ca*) for photos and information. There is more about the Brant Wildlife Festival at *www.brantfestival.bc.ca*.

Burrowing Owl by Wayne MacDonald. Best of Show, Wildlife, Novice.

Wood Duck by Jim Price. Best of Show, Wildlife, Intermediate.

Pacific Brant by Vern Jones. Best Brant.

Pacific Brant by Vern Jones. Second Best of Division, Realistic Life-size, Expert.

Steller's Jay by Dieter Golze. First, Miniature Landbirds, Expert.

Spruce Grouse by Jack Tucker. Cabela's Award.

Wigeon by Roy Koyama.
Best Antique-style Ducks.

Greater Yellowlegs by Bill Beese.
Best Antique-style Shorebirds.

Green-winged Teal Drake by Malcom Ho-You.
Cabela's Award.

Pacific Brant by Bob Lavender.
Best Cocktail Bird (Air).

Common Merganser Hen by Harvey Welch.
Best Hunting Decoy.

QUINTE WOODCARVERS COMPETITION AND SHOW

April 8, 2017: Belleville, Ontario

Text by Robert Danahy

Photography by Ken McKenzie

The year 2017 marked the 30th Anniversary of Quinte Woodcarvers. To celebrate, carvers and visitors at the competition and show in April were treated to cake and drinks. Even better, everyone who came to the show received the chance to see a wide range of excellent wildfowl carvings.

Larry Fell walked away with top honors in the open class, winning best in show in the decorative floating category with his Pacific brant goose. (Larry's brant went on to win best in world pairs at the Ward show, and you can see it on page 64.) Best of show in floating decoys went to Dave Ricci and his hooded merganser. (This bird was also a winner at the Canadian Nationals show; see page 45). Wendy Hatch won best of show in decorative wildfowl with her beautiful carving of an oriole weaving a nest. Intermediate winners included Serge Moisan, Linda Gawel, and Laurie Snelling, while T. Wayne Lawson and Sue Pratt scored at the novice level.

You can find more details about the 2017 competition and see the winning carvings in each category at the club website, *www.quintewoodcarvers.ca*. The 2018 Competition and Show is scheduled for April 7 in Belleville.

Baltimore Oriole by Wendy Hatch. Best of Show, Decorative Wildfowl, Open.

American Kestrel by Warren Townsend. First, Birds of Prey, Open.

Trogon by Mary Beckstead. First, Decorative Others, Open.

Ring-necked Drake by Serge Moison. Best of Show, Decorative Floating, Intermediate.

American Robin by Sue Pratt. Best of Show, Decorative Wildfowl, Novice.

Hooded Merganser Drake by T. Wayne Lawson. Best of Show, Decorative Floating, Novice.

PRAIRIE CANADA CARVING CHAMPIONSHIP

April 22 – 23, 2017: Winnipeg, Manitoba

Text by Ted Muir

Photography by Richard Gwizdak

For its 31st annual show, the Prairie Canada Carving Championship relocated to the Pembina Curling Club in Winnipeg. The change of location, from a hotel conference center to a curling rink in the ice-free season, provided a spacious, well-lit venue at a reasonable cost and was warmly received by all.

Austin Eade of Craig, Saskatchewan, claimed best of show at the open level with a female pine grosbeak. Second best of show went to Reuben Unger of Clavet, Saskatchewan, for a life-size cooper's hawk. Susan Cowtan of Winnipeg made her presence known by clinching a third best of show, open,

with a green-winged teal hen and a first in cocktail waterfowl with a redhead hen. In the purchase award category, she captured the Richard Whittom Duck Head Award with a canvasback hen and the Jim Richardson Antique Canadian Duck Award with a W. J. Crawford bluebill.

At the intermediate level, Cheryl Laschuk of Seddons Corner, Manitoba, won first with an American crow. Gerald Lukianchuk of Keewatin, Ontario, took a second with a male ruby-throated hummingbird, and Prabir Mitra of Winnipeg captured third with a common loon. Carrie Braden of Portage la Prairie, Manitoba, cleaned house in

Green-winged Teal Hen by Susan Cowtan.
Third Best of Show, Open.

Pine Grosbeak by Austin Eade.
Best of Show, Open.

novice with a first-place bufflehead drake, a second-place ruddy duck drake, and a third-place miniature northern pintail drake. Her efforts also won her the Oak Hammock Marsh Carving Guild-Don Phalen Award.

In the purchase award category Tom Park of Winnipeg won the Razertip Industries raffle piece award with a common redpoll. Tom also claimed a first in cocktail wading birds with an American flamingo. Ray Minaudier of St. Claude, Manitoba, walked away with the Morgan Whiteway BOSS award with a ring-necked duck drake, while Ray's cinnamon teal pair earned him the Carvers' Choice award sponsored by Adanac Carvers Association. Birkley Ross of Lac du Bonnet, Manitoba, won the Prairie Canada Junior award, sponsored by Cliff Zarecki, for a rusty nail shorebird.

On the traditional carving table, Bill Nitzsche of Barrier Bay, Manitoba, took open best of show with a stylized family of birds. This piece also claimed the People's Choice award, sponsored by Les Gens de Bois Woodcarving Club. Shirley Lawrence of Winnipeg won second in open with her common loon, and William Novak of Winnipeg took first in novice for his stylized swans. Murray Watson of Winnipeg won first in traditional cocktail carvings with a Canada goose.

An interesting array of workshops figured prominently in the show, ranging in length from four hours to a day and half. Topics included habitat design and construction by Tom Park, wood burning by Louise Reilly, wood spirit carving by Paul Giasson, English paper piercing by Marie Minaudier, chainsaw carving by Russ Kubara, fish painting by Jean Mousseau, and bronze finishing by Doug Danell. Show judge Randy Mooi delivered the keynote address at the awards banquet with an illustrated presentation on the natural history and demise of the passenger pigeon—at one point the most abundant bird in the world. Ted Muir received the Carvers' Award of Excellence at the banquet for his years of service to the carving community.

The 2018 competition will take place at the Pembina Curling Club on April 21 and 22. For information about the show, go to *www.prairiecanadacarvers.com* or contact Tom Park at *tpark@mts.net* or (204) 269-4290.

American Crow by Cheryl Laschuck. Best of Show, Intermediate.

American Flamingo by Tom Park. First, Wading Birds, Cocktail Bird.

Bufflehead Drake by Carrie Braden. Best of Show, Novice.

Rusty Nail Shorebird by Birkley Ross. First, Junior Cash Award.

Common Redpoll by Tom Park. Razertip 2018 Raffle Piece Purchase Award.

Ring-necked Duck Drake by Ray Minaudier. Morgan Whiteway BOSS Purchase Award.

Swans by William Novak. Best of Show, Traditional Carvers, Novice.

*Canada Goose by Murray Watson. First,
Traditional Carvings, Cocktail Bird.*

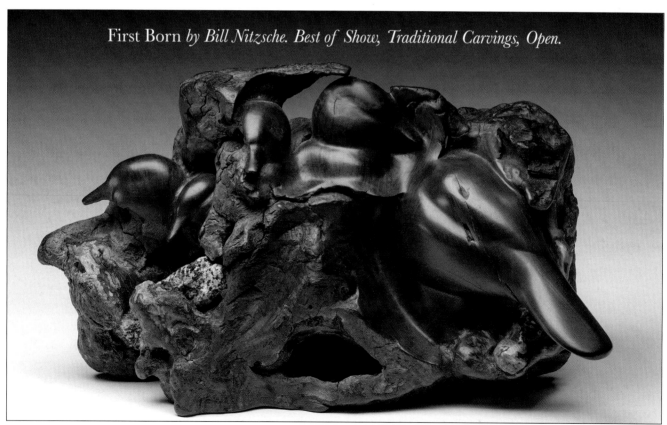

First Born by Bill Nitzsche. Best of Show, Traditional Carvings, Open.

Reuben Unger was destined to become a champion bird carver from his days growing up on a family dairy farm in Hague, Saskatchewan. He fondly recalls wandering the countryside as a youngster in search of birds, counting the eggs in each discovered nest. "Whatever sparked that love for nature, it stayed with me all my life," says Reuben. Not surprisingly, his penchant for all things wild led him to become a self-taught, part-time taxidermist. However, the realities of having to make a decent living sent Reuben on what became a 37-year career with the Saskatchewan potash industry as a safety professional. Thirteen years before retiring in 1998, Reuben visited a wildlife art competition in Saskatoon, Saskatchewan, and realized that he needed to try his hand at bird carving. "I think my love for nature and exposure to woodworking through my father, who was an accomplished furniture maker and wood turner, led me to carving, and I have not turned back," he says.

Reuben's entry into the world of competitive carving in 1999 was a humbling experience. "I realized how awful my first bird looked compared to other novice entries, and quickly sought help from local carvers," he says. Luckily, he lived among some of the best in the nation. With instruction from the likes of Leroy Royer, Cam Merkle, Harvey Welch, and Bob Lavender, Reuben became a serious competitor. It wasn't long before he was raking in best of show awards from all the major bird carving shows in western Canada.

For the most part, Reuben likes to carve alone, gleaning information from study skins, study bills, photographs, and articles from WILDFOWL CARVING MAGAZINE. "I find WILDFOWL CARVING MAGAZINE an invaluable resource," he says. Reuben works from sketches to guide his work and, unlike many of his peers, he enjoys painting, not a sentiment shared by most bird carvers.

In 2015, Reuben fulfilled a long-time goal and attended the Ward World Championship in Maryland, where he earned a third best of show in intermediate with a life-sized brown creeper. In 2016, after recovering from a heart attack, he took his dream workshop from Floyd Scholz at Krausman's Studio in Michigan. "I was like a kid in a candy store for 10 full days as we carved a life-sized Cooper's hawk," he recalls. "It was the experience of a lifetime." That same year he was honored as featured artist at the Saskatchewan Reflections of Nature Art Show and Sale. In 2017 he went back to the Worlds and captured a first in miniature in intermediate for a great gray owl. That same year he won a second best of show open at Prairie Canada for a life-size Cooper's hawk. He carves about six major pieces a year and his birds have found homes as far away as Sweden and Texas.

Reuben advocates participating in competitions as a means of improving oneself, noting that all carvings look good sitting at home. He also values competitions for the friendships they create. He has stepped up his game by judging shows in Winnipeg and Saskatoon. Reuben is also a firm believer in the value of helping others less fortunate and using art to give back to the community. Each year he donates proceeds from carving sales to charitable organizations like the Saskatchewan Wildlife Federation and the Nature Conservancy of Canada.

In his spare time, Reuben enjoys wetting a line in various northern Saskatchewan lakes and streams with his wife, Kathy. After all these years he still draws inspiration from outdoor excursions. We can only hope that he continues to channel it through art.

Cooper's Hawk by Reuben Unger. Second Best of Show, Open.

Scaup Drake by Susan Cowtan. Jim Richardson Antique Canadian Decoy Purchase Award.

Redhead Hen by Susan Cowtan. First in Waterfowl, Cocktail Bird.

Canvasback Hen by Susan Cowtan. Richard Whittom Duck Head Purchase Award.

Common Loon by Shirley Lawrence. Second Best of Show, Traditional Carvings, Open.

WARD WORLD CHAMPIONSHIP

April 28 – 30, 2017: Ocean City, Maryland

Text by Shaina Adkins

Photography by Alan Wycheck, Courtesy the Ward Museum

Blue Jay by Thomas Horn. First, Feathers.

Cape Sugarbird Pair by Gerald Painter. Best in World Miniature Wildfowl.

Purple Heron by Gary Eigenberger. Second Best in World Miniature Wildfowl.

Camaraderie and creativity were everywhere at the 47th Annual Ward World Championship, as carvers from more than 15 countries gathered at the Roland E. Powell Convention Center in Ocean City, Maryland. This year the competitors had two new outlets for their creativity, feathers and palm fronds. The palm fronds division, a long-requested addition, was dedicated to the late Bob Sutton, who had promoted this unique kind of carving during his years of advocacy for bird carving. Dozens of competitors used the division as a way to honor Bob and his dedication to the carving world.

The classes offered by the World Competition Education Conference provided a variety of exciting opportunities for carvers of all ages and skill sets. Students learned about everything from practical carving tips to design theory while hearing stories from experienced professionals of the carving world. Among the teachers this year were Rich and Ross Smoker, Laurie Truehart, and Laurie McNeil, to name just a few.

Griffon Vulture by Jeff Krete. Third Best in World Miniature Wildfowl.

The 2017 competition highlighted artwork from some of the best carvers in the world, with Lynn Branson, Larry Fell, Gary Eigenberger, Keith Mueller, and Gerald Painter winning top honors at the world level.

Lynn Branson took best in world in the interpretive wood sculpture division with a carving of a brown pelican she titled *Emergence*. "The wood just said pelican, and that's how I've always worked," said Branson. "The wood always tells me what it wants to be." This was her fourth win in the interpretive division.

Larry Fell's single white-fronted goose won in the decorative life-size wildfowl pair division. It was Larry's first best in world title. He carved the goose from tupelo and spent nearly 500 hours creating and perfecting it. Larry has been coming to the Ward World Championship for 26 years, and he says he always finds inspiration at the show. He cites Paul Burdette and Glenn McMurdo as influences.

Gary Eigenberger, a regular in the winner's circle in Ocean City, took his first best in world in the decorative life-size wildfowl division with a reddish egret he made from tupelo. The beautiful plumes of a reddish egret he and his wife spotted at Florida's Ding Darling Nature Center provided inspiration, and Gary worked on the piece on and off for about five months. He says herons and egrets are favorite carving subjects.

The winner of best in world shootin' rig was seven-time world champion Keith Mueller and his red phalaropes. Keith has been carving professionally for nearly 40 years, having learned in his early teens by painting a neighbor's duck decoys at the end of the season. Keith was inspired by the phalarope while cod fishing in the winter months. "It's a joy to watch this small seabird effortlessly riding the large swells far out from the shore," he says.

Gerald Painter is no stranger to Ocean City either, but 2017 marked the first time he's won best in world since he first attended the show in 2008. He has won second and third before, but this year his pair of Cape sugarbirds won top honors in the miniature division. "I always look for a challenge when doing a World entry," he says. "Long tails and thin beaks are a challenge to do in a miniature. Add to that some crazy difficult habitat and that's my kind of piece."

The 2017 show was another great year for the youth competition, with more than 150 entries from both the United States and Canada. Peter Palumbo is providing the silhouette pattern for the 2018 youth competition, and it can be downloaded from the Ward Museum's website.

Congratulations to all of the winners of the 2017 show! For more information on how you can be more involved at the 2018 competition, visit *www.wardmuseum.org*.

White-fronted Goose by Larry Fell. Best in World Decorative Life-size Waterfowl Pair.

White-fronted Goose by Rick Bobincheck. Second Best in World Decorative Life-size Waterfowl Pair.

White-fronted Goose by Anthony Donato. Third Best in World Decorative Life-size Waterfowl Pair.

Reddish Egret by Gary Eigenberger. Best in World Decorative Life-size Wildfowl.

Cape May Warblers by Joshua Guge. Second in World Decorative Life-size Wildfowl.

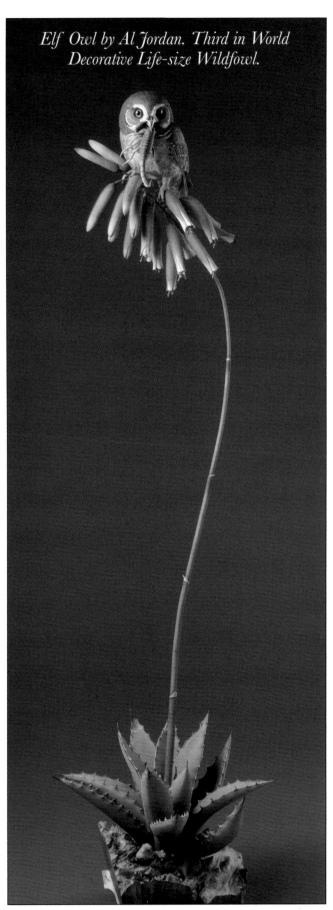

Elf Owl by Al Jordan. Third in World Decorative Life-size Wildfowl.

Brown Pelican by Lynn Branson. Best in World Interpretive Wood Sculpture.

Hawk by Tom Baldwin. Second Best in World Interpretive Wood Sculpture.

Flying into Extinction by Daniel Montano. Third Best in World Interpretive Wood Sculpture.

Phalaropes by Keith Mueller. Best in World, Jimmy Vizier Memorial Award (Shootin' Rig).

Canvasbacks and Swan by Thomas Flemming. Second Best in World Shootin' Rig.

*Gadwalls by Tom Christie.
Third in World Shootin' Rig*

*Bufflehead by Kent Duff. First in Master's
Decorative Life-size Floating Waterfowl.*

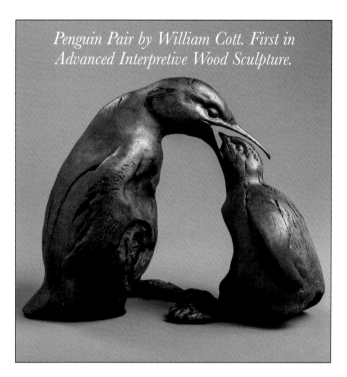

Penguin Pair by William Cott. First in Advanced Interpretive Wood Sculpture.

Blue-tailed Bee Eaters by Gary Eigenberger. First in Master's Decorative Miniature Wildfowl.

Rough-legged Hawk by Gary Eigenberger. First in Master's Decorative Life-size Wildfowl.

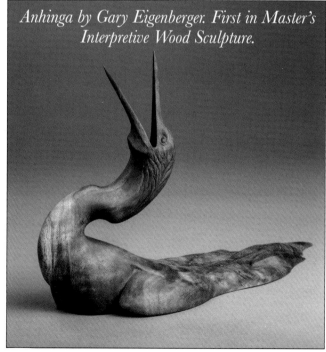

Anhinga by Gary Eigenberger. First in Master's Interpretive Wood Sculpture.

*Brant by Mike Amaral.
Lem & Steve Best in
Division, Contemporary Decoy.*

Grebe by Ted Smith. Lem & Steve Champagne
Waterfowl Champion.

Cormorant by Peter Johnson. Lem & Steve
Best in Division, Champagne Waterfowl.

Eiders by Luke Costilow. Lem & Steve Gunning Pair Champion.

Shovelers by Chris Martin. Lem & Steve Best in Division, Gunning Pair.

Wren by Greg Pedersen. First in Advanced Decorative Life-size Wildfowl.

Ring-necked Pheasants by Pat Moore. First in Advanced Decorative Miniature Wildfowl.

Hooded Merganser Drake by Joe Tamborra. First in Advanced Decorative Life-size Floating Waterfowl.

The 2017 Living Legends were (left to right) Bennett Scott, Curt Fabre, and Tom Christie

In 2017, the Ward Museum of Wildfowl Art recognized three more artists as Living Legends. Honorees Tom Christie, Curt Fabre, and Bennett Scott have all proved themselves generous in teaching and passing on their knowledge, skills, and talents, and have created an impact on the field of wildfowl art and/or the Ward World Championship competition.

Tom Christie (b. 1956) grew up in Marion, Indiana, and developed a fascination with wildfowl at an early age, through hunting with his father on the Tippecanoe River. He began carving his own hunting decoys in 1986, when he made three goldeneyes to add to his rig. Membership in the Maumee Bay Carvers introduced him to competitive carving and he won his first best of show in 1989. Since then, Tom has won numerous carving competitions across the country. He is a six-time Ward World Champion in the shootin' rig category, has eight best in show awards in the Lem & Steve Ward competition, and is a nine-time IWCA International Wildfowl Carving Association National Champion. Tom also enjoys teaching seminars and judging at various shows. In addition, he has volunteered for wildfowl carving organizations and competitions across the country, including service on the Ward World Championship Rules Committee.

Born and raised in southern Louisiana, Curt Fabre (b. 1929) hunted over his family's hand-carved decoys in the marshes of the bayou country. By the late 1970s, he learned to create highly detailed competition birds. In the early 1980s, Curt started supplying carvers with tools and wood through his business, Curt's Waterfowl Corner. But he provides more than materials; fellow carvers say Curt has an uncanny ability to educate himself on the methods and tools used by the best wildfowl carvers, and then to teach that knowledge to beginners. As a carver himself, Curt has won awards, including best in category at the Ward, a life membership in the Waterfowl Preservation and Decoy Club of Michigan, person of the year from the Northern Nationals in Minnesota, and lifetime achievement awards from the South Louisiana Wildfowl Carvers, Louisiana Wildfowl Carvers, and Collectors Guild. He describes bird carvers as "an honorable and trusting group with a lot in common: a passion for nature and birds, a desire to create, and a willingness to help and share with others." Curt Fabre certainly fits that mold.

Bennett Scott (b. 1942) grew up in Berlin, Maryland, and was raised on the family farm that he still owns today. His interest in carving was born out of his love for nature and for hunting. Bennett is recognized as a leading wildfowl carver, having won numerous awards at shows throughout the Mid-Atlantic. He began carving to pass time at work in the 1960s, at first with miniatures. In 1970 he participated in his first decoy contest, in Chincoteague, Virginia, and won a best in show ribbon the next year. He started competing at the Ward Competition in 1974, eventually winning in the Lem and Steve Ward shootin' stool category. The key to his success is to never be satisfied. He can always find something in a decoy that he would have done differently, which drives him to improve the next. Bennett also helps pass carving traditions to the next generation—including as a master carver in the Carving Out Future Decoy Makers program. He also volunteers extensively, including judging at the Ward World Championship and the Chesapeake Wildfowl Expo, and serving on both competitions' organizing committees, and on the Ward Foundation's board of directors. He was inducted into the Easton Waterfowl Festival Hall of Fame in 2003.

Common Eider Hen by Daniel Montano. First, Palm Fronds.

Pintail by Tom Christie. Third, Palm Fronds.

Oystercatcher by Bruce DiVaccaro. Lem & Steve Best in Division, Shorebird Decoy.

California Condor by Daniel Montano. Second, Palm Fronds.

Semipalmated Plover by Peter Palumbo. Lem & Steve Best in Division, Smoothie Shorebirds and Wading Birds.

Dove by Dana Kelman. First, Youth Silhouette 1.

Dove by Dannie Montano. First, Youth Silhouette 2.

Rose-breasted Grosbeak by Kage Guge. First, Decorative Wildfowl 3.

Warbler by Jonathan Irons. First, Yourth Decorative Wildfowl 2.

Great Crested Grebe by Joe Tamborra. Lem & Steve Best in Division, Decorative Smoothie Waterfowl.

Canvasback Drake by Donovan Shockley. First, Youth Gunning Decoy 2.

PACIFIC FLYWAY DECOY CLASSIC

July 22 – 23, 2017: Sacramento, California

Text by Jim Burcio

Photography by Rob Solari

Wigeon Drake by Brad Snodgrass. First, Decorative Life-size Floating, Open.

To kick off the 47th annual Pacific Flyway Decoy Classic, held in Sacramento, California, last July, a room full of carvers, collectors, artists, and vendors gathered for the Friday evening cocktail party and auction of miniature carvings.

The judging began on Saturday. Anthony Donato was one of the big winners, capturing best of show in floating decoratives and the coveted Troon Award with his white-fronted goose (see page 64). Del Herbert's Richardson's goose took best of show for PFDA traditional hunting decoys. Rounding out the floating categories, Tom Christie topped all entries in the contemporary decoy competition with a gadwall.

Gary De Cew took the blue ribbon in field decoys with a mourning dove. Brock Hinton won best of show for decorative life-size with a blue-winged teal, while Gerald Painter's willow ptarmigan took top honors in decorative miniatures. Peter Palumbo continued his winning ways out west with a best of show greater yellowlegs.

This year's three-bird rig consisted of a green-winged teal hen and drake combination judged from a distance in Suisun Marsh one month before the show, with the top five rigs advancing to the tanks. Roger Anderson took top honors for the second straight year. The international waterfowl competition featured three sponsor-selected species. Walter Gaskill continued his winning ways with a ringed teal. Walter also took top honors with redheads in the California Rice Commission competition and California Waterfowl Association's Decoy of the Year competition. But he wasn't done yet, as he topped all entries in the sea duck challenge with a spectacled eider. Gary De Cew's blue-ribbon American avocet completed the California Rice Commission's second category.

The PFDA enjoys a wide variety of sponsored purchase awards. The featherweight event features a unique balance of serviceability, portability, and artistry. Tom Matus's blue-winged teal took top honors. Joe Girtner earned the right of first selection in the six-inch swap decoy with his wood duck, while Jerry Harris's wood duck won the mini decoy competition. The U.S. Fish and Wildlife competitions went to Don Hovie's California quail and Gary Smoot's condor head. R.D. Wilson prevailed once again with a best of show in the always-popular doubtful antiques with a canvasback.

In a continuing effort to "keep it fun," the show's most creative carvers received a new challenge. The task was to carve an umagooli—a very rare shorebird that has never been photographed. Known only to be "about the size of a curlew, with a down-turned beak and unusually short legs," the bird is known to scream "umagooli" as it enters the ice-cold waters of Loch Ness. The table full of entries was the center of discussion for the entire weekend. Showing how unusual thoughts can lead to an unusual entry, R. D. Wilson claimed the top prize.

Look for more innovative categories at the Pacific Flyway Decoy Classic's 48th show, scheduled for July 21–22, 2018. For more information, check out the website at *www.pacificflyway.org*.

Greater Yellowlegs by Peter Palumbo. Best of Show, Bob Peterson Gunning Shorebirds, Open; First, Willets and Yellowlegs.

California Valley Quail by Don Hovie. First, U.S. Fish and Wildlife Competition.

Green-winged Teal by Terry Avila. Third Best of Show, Decorative Life-size Floating, Open.

Barn Owl by Gary Smoot. First, Decorative Life-size Wildfowl (Raptors), Open.

Gadwall Drake by Tom Christie. Best of Show, Contemporary Decoys, Open.

Green-winged Teal by Roger Anderson. First, CWA Three-bird Rig.

Richardson's Goose by Del Herbert. Best of Show, PFDA Traditional Hunting Decoys, Open.

American Avocet by Del Herbert. First, Bob Peterson Gunning Shorebirds, Open.

Blue-winged Teal by Tom Matus. First, Featherweight Decoys.

California Condor Head by Gary Smoot. First, U.S. Fish & Wildlife Competition.

Blue-winged Teal by Brock Hinton. Best of Show, Decorative Life-size Wildfowl (Waterfowl), Open.

Redhead Drake by Walter Gaskill. CWA Decoy of the Year.

Redhead Drake by Walter Gaskill. First, California Rice Commission.

California Quail by Larry Woods. First, Decorative Life-size Wildfowl (Upland Game), Open.

Ringed Teal by Walter Gaskill. First, International Waterfowl.

Mourning Dove by Gary De Cew. First, Field or Stick Up Decoys, Open.

American Avocet by Gary De Cew. First, California Rice Commission.

Willow Ptarmigan by Gerald Painter. Best of Show, Decorative Miniature Wildfowl Carvings, Open.

Canvasback by R.D. Wilson. Best of Show, Doubtful Antiques.

Umagooli by R.D. Wilson. Best of Show, Umagooli.

For Brad Snodgrass, the combination of his grandfather's decoys, a balsa life raft he found on an Alaskan beach, and the mentoring of Dennis Schroeder led to a steady improvement in his work, more ribbons at shows, and his growing recognition as a top carver.

His grandfather lived in the Illinois River area, and hunted with decoys created by some of the best carvers of that region. "We'd go out hunting over these beautiful wooden decoys," Brad says. "Eventually people started telling us you shouldn't be shooting holes in them."

The life raft entered the picture after Brad went to Alaska for a teaching job. While waiting for school to start, he earned money digging clams and found the raft on the beach. He used a chain saw to turn it into "the world's worst looking decoys" in time for hunting season. They didn't look pretty, but something about the way they floated attracted ducks. (He lost most of those decoys years later when a tidal bore swamped his boat in Alaska.)

As a high school principal, Brad attended a conference in San Diego, but ended up playing hooky to attend the California Open show. He was determined to exploit Alaska's attractions to lure a carving teacher north. He liked the way that Dennis Schroeder was critiquing work at the show, so he introduced himself. "I'm from Alaska," Brad said. "Do you like to fish?" Schroeder did, and he accepted the invitation to teach a carving seminar. The two men later ended up living across from each other and carving together in California. Brad calls Schroeder his "mentor."

Brad cites a quote from Winston Churchill that success is an ability to endure a long string of failures without ever losing enthusiasm. "That's the story of my carving," he says. Initially he found himself dreading painting. "Dennis helped me get past that." He started with oils, but switched to acrylics and an airbrush. The airbrush is not magic, he says. It's just another tool. "What a lot of people don't understand about the airbrush is that it's not as much about the airbrush as it is about the stenciling. It's about the negative space that you leave, as opposed to where the paint goes. And then the ability to move on and disguise that with a real brush."

Brad uses mostly power tools. "I'll use the tool that works for the job," he says. "But it doesn't mean you have to criticize those of us who carve with power tools, and it doesn't mean that those of us who carve with power tools can't use a knife. I can use a knife."

He's tried lots of woods, but prefers tupelo and is in the fortunate position of having a steady supply. Several years ago, Schroeder received a call from a woman whose husband had died and left six pallets of tupelo. "He and I bought it all," Brad says. "When that's all carved, we're done."

That will take a while. "I've still got a long way to go," Brad says. "Every carving's a new adventure."

Cinnamon Teal Drake by Brad Snodgrass. First, Decorative Life-size Floating, Open.

BIRDS IN ART

September 9 – November 26, 2017: Wausau, Wisconsin

Majestic Presence (2017) by Thomas J. Horn. Acrylic on tupelo and brass.

American Bittern (2017) by Larry Barth. Acrylic on tupelo.

More than 100 artists from around the world displayed their work at the 42nd annual "Birds in Art" exhibition at the Leigh Yawkey Woodson Art Museum. Of those, 94 were artists whose work was selected by three jurors who reviewed more than 800 entries. Among the exhibitors were some of the top names in the field of wildfowl carving.

Larry Barth returned to "Birds in Art" with an American bittern inspired by one he had seen captured at a banding station. "When we released the bird in an open field, rather than making a hasty exit, it drew itself upright and stood its ground, adopting the characteristic motionless stance bitterns use to avoid detection," Barth said. "This sculpture is based on sketches I made as the bird very, very, very slowly walked away."

Wisconsin native Gary Eigenberger's contribution was a rough-legged hawk. He titled the piece *Winter's Arrival* and recalled that while driving throughout Wisconsin he often saw the hawks, "perched low to the ground in open farm country watching attentively for prey. These are birds I see in late fall and winter. Working on this sculpture sparked memories of these sightings, which suggested the title."

Patrick Godin carved a pair of Barrow's goldeneyes, a species he has seen in the wild only once but one he's long wanted to carve, especially the hen. "I designed the two pieces to complement each other," he explained. "The focal point is the drake's lifted, orange-yellow foot, which ties him to the hen with her bright yellow-orange bill. My goal in painting is not only to match the color pigmen-

Canadian Breakfast *(2015) by John T. Sharp. Black cherry.*

Winter's Arrival *(2017) by Gary Eigenberger. Oil on tupelo and lilac.*

DIANE EIGENBERGER

tation of the bird, but also to incorporate the illusion of light falling on the surface to enhance the dimension and add drama."

With his sculpture of an American kestrel and a collared lizard, Josh Guge was as interested in the reptile as the bird. Rather than use wood for the delicate lizard, he soldered a thin brass armature for the arms and tail, then covered it with epoxy and carved that. "While the process was delicate and time consuming, it's a new technique I'll use again," he said.

Tomas Horn called his sculpture of a violet sabrewing hummingbird *Majestic Presence*. When he saw the bird in Costa Rica, he thought it was "by far the most impressive hummingbird I've ever seen. Its size, royal purple color, and white-tipped tail gave it a regal appearance as it flew past the equally beautiful orchids." It was, Horn said, "a sight I will cherish forever."

Gerald Painter also submitted a hummingbird, a booted racket-tail, and he called the resulting sculpture *Puffleg*. "Its iridescent plumage, distinctive tail shape, and feathered legs—little 'powder puffs' around the feet—cannot be overlooked," he said. Painter typically sculpts North American birds but he "embraced the challenge" of this South American species "by creating a habitat that would be interesting and harmonious without overpowering the little gem of a bird." To hint at the bird's threatened habitat, he carved the bottom of the stump to look like a chainsaw cut.

"A hunting buddy and I often conclude a trip afield or on the water with a 'Canadian breakfast,' a six pack of beer and a bag of potato chips," said John Sharp, explaining the title of his sculpture. "I blackened the bird with an ink wash for contrast and brightened the bottles with spar varnish."

For more information, visit *www.lywam.org*, e-mail the Museum at *museum@lywam.org*, or call (715) 845-7010.

A 134-page, full-color, illustrated "Birds in Art" catalog, featuring every artwork along with artists' statements, is available for purchase. You can order catalogues at www.lywam.org/catalogues.

Barrow's Goldeneye Pair (2016) by Patrick Godin. Acrylic on tupelo and dogwood.

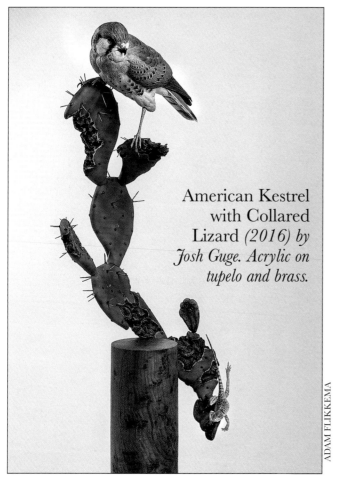

American Kestrel with Collared Lizard *(2016) by Josh Guge. Acrylic on tupelo and brass.*

ADAM FLIKKEMA

Puffleg (2017) by Gerald J. Painter. Acrylic on holly, walnut, and brass.

THE STUDIO, PETER VANCE

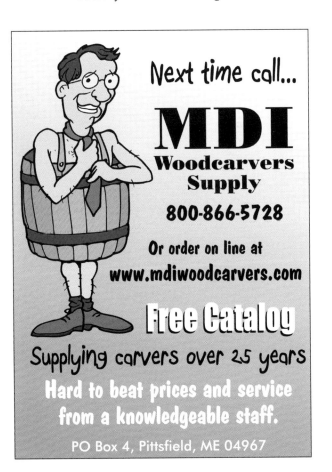

COLUMBIA FLYWAY WILDLIFE SHOW

September 9 – 10, 2017: Vancouver, Washington

Text by Donald Baiar

Photography by Matt Furcron

American Kestrel by Ted Smith.
First Best of Division, Open.

Wile the fire-ravaged Columbia Gorge Highway was closed, and forest fires throughout central Oregon somewhat dampened turnout, many intrepid and faithful carvers managed to reach Vancouver, Washington, and compete in another great Columbia Flyway Wildlife Show in 2017. This was the 30th anniversary show, and once again the city of Vancouver joined the Feather & Quill Carvers to host the "Northwest Championship" at the city's spectacular Water Resources Education Center.

Jerry Simchuk was the featured carver this year, and he had a quality display. On Friday Jerry provided an informative discussion and demonstration on the topic of "Artistry and Competition" in the center's classroom. (Jerry also earned a best of division and the Saturday people's choice award for an exquisite scrub jay that he has been documenting in three issues of WILDFOWL CARVING MAGAZINE.) Professional taxidermist Mike Monroe gave an informative Saturday demonstration on preparing study skins as carving and painting resources. On Sunday morning, expert carver Brad Snodgrass gave an excellent presentation about "Thinking Outside the Pond," with many valuable tips on getting reference material, making patterns, and painting. Brad also filled in as auctioneer at the banquet.

Judy Caldwell won another best of show honor as she swept the mammals division, with a stunningly realistic bust of a pronghorn antelope that also took home the chairman's choice award. Her wonderful pair of otters received the Water Resources Center award. Perennial show favorite Ted Smith won the coveted carvers' choice award with an entrancing little grebe. The Audubon award and Sunday people's choice were deservedly bagged by Steve Reed for a remarkably detailed preening hooded merganser on a log.

The Feather & Quill $500 purchase award went to Jerry Harris for his superb IWCA-style redhead drake. Sandee Johnson's exceptional Steller's jay earned her the mayor's award, while Del Herbert's fine mallard hen decoy took home a best of division and the $1,000 Drennan purchase award. Tom Matus impressed the Ducks Unlimited award judges with a wonderful working pintail hen decoy.

Rick Pass's merganser won the Will Hayden memorial amateur award, with Andrew Speer's grebe in second, and Larry Crist's black-necked stilt taking third. In the popular 6″ mini-wigeon trader floating decoy event, Tom Jones, Ted Smith, and Don Baiar came in first through third, respectively. Next year's species for this event will be the bufflehead drake.

This year the show hosted the IWCA working decoy championship. Tom Matus's variety of quality entries swept many of the species categories, and his merganser took first overall and his gadwall won third. Second place went to David Luoma's stately cormorant.

The dates for the 2018 show are September 8-9. Keep an eye on the website, *www.columbiaflywaywild-lifeshow.com* for periodic updates, show brochure, photos, entry forms, rules, and contact info. You can also like the show's Facebook page.

Scrub Jay by Jerry Simchuk. First Best of Division, Open; Saturday People's Choice.

Least Bittern by Robert Chiavarini. First in Open.

Steller's Jay by Sandee Johnson. Mayor's Choice Award.

Yellow-headed Blackbird by Paul Foshay. First in Open.

Red-breasted Merganser Hen by Rick Pass. First, Will Hayden Memorial Award.

Black-necked Stilt by Larry Crist. Third, Will Hayden Award.

Grebe by Andrew Speer. Second, Will Hayden Memorial Award.

Pintail Hen by Tom Matus. Ducks Unlimited Award.

Hooded Merganser by Steve Reed. Audubon Award; Sunday People's Choice; First, IWCA Decorative Life-size Waterfowl, Open.

Mallard Hen by Del Herbert. $1,000 Best of IWCA-style Drennan Purchase Award; Best of Division, IWCA-style Decoy.

Redhead Drake by Jerry Harris. $500 Feather & Quill Club Purchase Award.

Little Grebe by Ted Smith. First Best of Division; Carvers' Choice Award.

Screech Owl by Sherry Klein. First Best of Division, Intermediate.

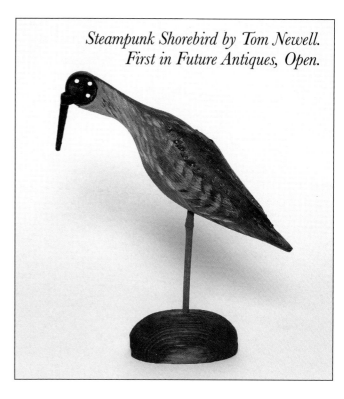

Steampunk Shorebird by Tom Newell. First in Future Antiques, Open.

Black Duck by Royce Embanks. Third in Future Antiques, Open.

Flamingo by Hank Wurgler. Best of Division, Intermediate.

Wood Duck Drake by Tom Newell. Second in Future Antiques, Open.

Miniature Screech Owl by Malcom Ho-You. Best of Division, Open.

Red-breasted Merganser Hen by Harold M. Brown. Best of Division, Novice.

Pintail Drake by Larry Harbaugh. Best of Division, Amateur.

Killdeer by Michael Donovan. Best of Division, Novice.

Miniature Trader Entries. Winners: Tom Jones, Ted Smith, and Don Baiar.

BRITISH DECOY & WILDFOWL CARVERS ASSOCIATION COMPETITION AND SHOW

September 9 – 10, 2017: Bakewell, Derbyshire, United Kingdom

Text by Pam Wilson

Photography by Frances Milburn

The Festival of Bird Art, the annual show of the British Decoy & Wildfowl Carvers Association (BDWCA), took place once again in the Agricultural Center in the picturesque town of Bakewell in Derbyshire. This is the only show of its kind in the United Kingdom and the competition is restricted to members at the youth, novice, intermediate, advanced, and open levels. However, there are also two non-membership competitions—the carved bird's head on a walking stick and the British Bird Carving Championship. The latter is the show's top award and competition is at the advanced level. The BDWCA introduced the championship 16 years ago in the hope of encouraging entries from outside the association, but nobody has taken up the challenge yet.

The quality of the entries continues to improve every year. For the first time, the top awards, including the British Bird Carving Championship, went to an interpretive wood sculpture. Claire Williams created this fascinating carving, which she entitled *Owl's Life*. The runner-up was a stretching stone curlew by Maggie Port, which also took the trophies for both visitor's and competitor's choices.

You will find more details about the winners and pictures of all the carvings entered in this year's show, as well as the winners from the previous three years, on the website at *www.bdwca.org.uk*. The 2018 competition and show will take place on September 8–9.

Hazel Hen by Richard Rossiter. Best Game Birds, Advanced.

Owl's Life by Claire Williams. Best Interpretive Wood Sculptures (Painted/Pyrographed); British Bird Carving Champion, BDWCA Champion, and BDWCA Best in Show.

Stone Curlew by Maggie Port. Best Sea Birds and Shore Birds, Advanced; Visitor's Choice; Competitor's Choice; Reserve Best in Show.

Sandwich Tern (Palm Frond) by Tom Fitzpatrick. Best Innovative Wildlife Sculpture, Open.

Winter Goosander by David Askew. Best Slick Smoothie Waterfowl, Advanced.

Sparrowhawk and Blackbird by Mike Wood. Best Bird of Prey, Advanced; Artistic Award.

Wigeon Drake by Dave Welham. Best Working Decoy, Open.

INTERNATIONAL WILDFOWL CARVERS ASSOCIATION

Text by Laurie J. McNeil

Common Merganser Drake by Robin Oliver. Best of Show, IWCA Canvas Decoy Championship.

BRENT HOOD

Looking back at 2017, we can say the International Wildfowl Carvers Association had a good year.

There were some changes. Tom Westbrock stepped down from the duties of treasurer after 11 years, and his wife, Darlene, ended her duties as membership chair after five years. The IWCA was fortunate to have Tom and Darlene help maintain and shape the organization as volunteers on the board, and wishes them well in their retirement.

Ray Brooks III of Daly City, California, stepped up to fill the position of membership chair. Ray has had a lifelong dedication to wildfowl carving, and his father was involved in the Pacific Flyway Decoy Association since its inception. Ray brings considerable experience to the organization and we are grateful to have him on the IWCA board of directors. The key position of treasurer has yet to be filled—the IWCA would love to hear from qualified people.

Last year also saw the introduction of a new affiliate member show. The Wisconsin Waterfowl Association held its first-ever decoy carving competition in Stevens Point, Wisconsin, in September.

All five of the IWCA Championship events took place in 2017 at affiliate member shows across the country. The Ohio Decoy Collectors and Carvers Association kicked off the competitions in March by hosting the IWCA Style Shorebird Championship in Strongsville. Bruce DiVaccaro of Sheffield Village, Ohio, won first best of show with an upland sandpiper and second with a Hudsonian godwit, for prizes of $200 and $100. Todd Van Wieren of Grand Ledge, Michigan, won third best of show and $50 with a marbled godwit.

The Core Sound Waterfowl Museum and Heritage Center in Harkers Island, North Carolina, hosted the IWCA Style Decoy Championship in June. Walter Gaskill of Beaufort, North Carolina, took first best of show and $200 with a lesser scaup hen, and third and $50 with a greater scaup drake. Jon Jones of Algonac, Michigan, won second (and $100) with a long-tailed duck drake.

The IWCA Working Decoy Championship took

Mallard Hen by Robin Oliver. Second Best of Show, IWCA Canvas Decoy Championship.

Bufflehead Drake by Robin Oliver. Third Best of Show, IWCA Canvas Decoy Championship.

BRENT HOOD (2)

place in September at the Columbia Flyway Wildlife Show in Vancouver, Washington. Tom Matus of Kuna, Idaho, took first and third (with prizes of $200 and $50) with two hens, a common merganser and a gadwall. David Luoma of Tillamook, Oregon, took second and the $100 prize with his cormorant.

The final championship competitions of the year unfolded at the Core Sound Decoy Festival in Harkers Island, North Carolina, in December. Robin Oliver went home with a sweep of the IWCA Canvas Championship, winning first, second and third best of show (for a total of $350 in prize money).

The winners in the Young Guns Championship were Sam Humphries (11 and under), Bray Lawrence (12–14) and Grayson Russell (15–17).

Decorative Carver of the Year at the Intermediate level went to Hank Wurgler of Anaheim, California, who accumulated a total of 455 points. Lisa Strang of Chocowinity, North Carolina, won the Novice level in the Decorative Carver of the Year with 80 points. Intermediate and novice carvers who enter into IWCA decorative divisions at the many IWCA affiliate member shows accumulate points over the year. The decorative carver with the most points wins top honors.

The IWCA encourages all carvers to attend the IWCA affiliate member shows throughout the year, volunteer to help at the shows, compete for prize money and ribbons sponsored by the IWCA, and, most of all, continue to carve and share their skills with everyone—young and old—to ensure the future of wildfowl and decoy carving. You can find the IWCA website at *www.iwfca.com.*

2018 IWCA CHAMPIONSHIP EVENTS

2018 IWCA STYLE SHOREBIRD CHAMPIONSHIP AND IWCA YOUNG GUNS. *September 8–9, 2018, at the Columbia Flyway Wildlife Show, Vancouver, Washington.*

2018 IWCA STYLE DECOY CHAMPIONSHIP AND IWCA WORKING DECOY CHAMPIONSHIP. *December 1–2, 2018, at the Core Sound Decoy Festival, Harkers Island, North Carolina.*

2018 DECORATIVE CARVER OF THE YEAR.

There will be no IWCA Canvas Decoy Championship in 2018. If you miss this event, please let the affiliate member shows know so they can arrange to host this championship in the future.

Upland Sandpiper by Bruce DiVaccaro. Best of Show, IWCA Style Shorebird Championship.

BRUCE RICHERT (3)

Common Merganser Hen by Tom Matus. Best of Show, IWCA Working Decoy Championship.

MATT FURGRON (3)

Hudsonian Godwit by Bruce DiVaccaro. Second Best of Show, IWCA Style Shorebird Championship.

Cormorant by David Luoma.. Second Best of Show, IWCA Working Decoy Championship.

Marbled Godwit by Todd Van Wieren. Third Best of Show, IWCA Style Shorebird Championship.

Gadwall Hen by Tom Matus. Third Best of Show, IWCA Working Decoy Championship.

Lesser Scaup Hen by Walter Gaskill. Best of Show, IWCA Style Decoy Championship.

PAM MORRIS (3)

Pintail Drake by Sam Humphries. Best of Show, Young Guns 11 and Under.

BRENT HOOD (3)

Long-tailed Duck Drake by Jon Jones. Second Best of Show, IWCA Style Decoy Championship.

Scaup Drake by Bray Lawrence. Best of Show, Young Guns 12–14.

Greater Scaup Drake by Walter Gaskill. Third Best of Show, IWCA Style Decoy Championship.

Bufflehead Hen by Grayson Russell. Best of Show, Young Guns 15–17.

BUY, SELL, TRADE

SUPPLIES

RAZERTIP PYROGRAPHIC TOOLS– World's finest, sharpest, most innovative burners. More information and free catalogue at www.razertip.com. See our ad on the back cover!

TUPELO–Light and white. No minimums. Cut to size. Ship UPS. Dealer inquiries welcome. Contact: Brad Ketrick, 105 Samantha Drive, Garner, NC 27529. Phone/fax: (919) 625-4070.

PUBLICATIONS

LOON AND CHICKS–by Laurie J. McNeil. The latest workbench project from Wildfowl Carving Magazine takes you step by step through the creation of an amazing loon sculpture. Order through our website, *www.wildfowl-carving.com.*

STILLER CARVING PATTERNS–Over 3000 carving patterns include Ducks, Geese, Shore Birds, Game Birds, Birds of Prey, Song Birds, Animals, Fish and Marine Animals. Colored patterns for birds and fish are also available. Gordon and Marsha Stiller started their business 33 years ago with the pattern inventory continually growing and new patterns being added each year. Check out our website *http://StillerPatterns.com* for our up-to-date schedule, and to view our online pattern catalog. Phone Orders: (920) 685-2938. E-mail: *gstiller2938@charter.net*. New Pictorial Catalog now available.

BACK ISSUES AND BOOKS– Missing any back issues of WILDFOWL CARVING MAGAZINE? The best way to fill in the gaps in your collection is by visiting our website, *www.wildfowl-carving.com*. Or you can call our toll-free number, (877) 762-8034. Canadian customers please call (866) 375-7257. This is also a great way to purchase our workbench projects or the amazing *Wings on the Water* and *Talons in the Sky* reference books. You can subscribe to the magazine or join our book club, too!

CLASSES, WORKSHOPS, & SEMINARS

KRAUSMAN'S WOODCARVING STUDIO 2018 SCHEDULE–Our 28th year in business, 19th year for seminars, 2018 promises to be the best yet here in the UP NORTH country where nature abounds. Our schedule will be exciting & challenging with teachers which include Keith Mueller, Pat Godin, Floyd Scholz, and Gary Eigenberger. You can now find our 2018 seminar schedule on our website. SIGN UP NOW to reserve your spot for 2018. The Krausmans started their business 28 years ago and now have over 300 sets of wildlife reference photos which include birds of prey, ducks, waterbirds, gamebirds, mammals, fish, & songbirds along with valuable measurements. Check out our website for complete details for 2018 & our listing of reference packets. Find us at *www.referencephotos.com* or call us toll-free at (877) 572-8762 for more information. Contact Pam & Jim Krausman at 1750 S Cty Rd 557, Gwinn, MI 49841, (906) 238-4475, or e-mail us at *jmkrausman@gmail.com*.

BUY/SELL/TRADE CLASSIFIED RATES

All classified ads must be PRE-PAID prior to each issue's deadline. Ads received late and accompanied by payment will be published in the following issue(s).

LISTING LENGTH	ONE TIME	FOUR TIMES
10-25 words	$40	$100
26-50 words	$55	$140
51-100 words	$85	$250
100+ words	$0.50 per word add'l	

[　] Check/Money Order (U.S. Funds Only)

[　] VISA　　[　] MasterCard

Credit Card No.

Exp. Date

Name:

Address:

City/State, Zip/Postal

Deadlines: Summer (July) issue, Apr. 5; Fall (Oct.) issue, July 12; Winter (Jan.) issue, Oct. 4; Spring (April) issue, Jan. 4: **Mail to:** Wildfowl Carving Magazine, 3400 Dundee Rd., Suite 220, Northbrook, IL 60062

INDEX TO ARTISTS

COMPETITION RESULTS

California Open Wildlife Arts Festival

PALM FROND CARVINGS

Decorative
1. Del Herbert
2. R.D. Wilson
3. Mike Dowell

Decoy Style
1. John Gewerth
2. Del Herbert
3. John Gewerth
HM. Daniel Montano

IWCA-STYLE DECOY, OPEN
1. Walter Gaskill
2. Tom Christie
3. Jon Jones

Puddle Ducks
1. Walter Gaskill
2. Tom Christie
3. John Gewerth

Mallard
1. Walter Gaskill
2. Terry Avila

Pintail
1. Tom Christie

Wigeon
1. John Gewerth
2. Vern Jones

All Teal
1. Charles Petersen

Shoveler
1. Edgar Frank

Diving Ducks
1. Walter Gaskill
2. Jon Jones
3. Edgar Frank

Merganser
1. Tom Christie
2. John Gewerth
3. Kenneth Crawford

Canvasback
1. Edgar Frank
2. Edgar Frank
3. Kenneth Crawford

Scaup
1. Walter Gaskill
2. Jon Jones
3. Charles Petersen

Confidence
1. Gary Joe Bryan

Geese
1. Edgar Frank
2. Robert Mueller

IWCA-STYLE DECOYS, AMATEUR
1. Steven Cogar
2. Steven Cogar
3. Don Combs

Puddle Ducks
1. James Higgins

All Teal
1. James Higgins

Diving Ducks
1. Steven Cogar
2. Steven Cogar
3. Don Combs

Goldeneye
1. Steven Cogar

Scaup
1. Don Combs
2. Michael Frechette
3. Michael Frechette

IWCA DECORATIVE LIFE-SIZE FLOATING, OPEN
1. Anthony Donato
2. Terry Avila
3. Leonard Rousseau

Puddle Ducks
1. Anthony Donato
2. Terry Avila
3. Leonard Rousseau

Diving Ducks
1. Leonard Rousseau
2. William Browne III

Geese and Confidence
1. Robert Mueller

IWCA DECORATIVE LIFE-SIZE FLOATING, INTERMEDIATE
1. Anthony Licciardello

Diving Ducks
1. Anthony Licciardello

IWCA DECORATIVE LIFE-SIZE NON-FLOATING, OPEN
1. Bunny Farley
2. Haruhiko Sakakura
3. Kazuo Nobe

Waterfowl
1. Bunny Farley
2. Malcolm Ho-You

Songbirds
1. Kazuo Nobe
2. Dale Steffen
3. Dale Steffen

Raptors
1. Haruhiko Sakakura

Miscellaneous
1. Bill Strickler

IWCA DECORATIVE LIFE-SIZE NON-FLOATING, INTERMEDIATE
1. Karen Hattman
2. Hank Wurgler
3. Hank Wurgler

Waterfowl
1. Hank Wurgler
2. Jim Price
3. Jim Price

Songbirds
1. Hank Wurgler
2. Hank Wurgler

Raptors
1. Hank Wurgler

Game Birds
1. Hank Wurgler
2. Hank Wurgler

Miscellaneous
1. Karen Hattman
2. Hank Wurgler
3. Hank Wurgler

IWCA DECORATIVE MINIATURE, OPEN
1. Gary De Cew
2. Leonard Rousseau
3. Walter Gaskill

IWCA DECORATIVE MINIATURES, INTERMEDIATE
1. Hank Wurgler
2. Hank Wurgler
3. Hank Wurgler

IWCA-STYLE SHOREBIRDS, OPEN
1. Gary Joe Bryan
2. Gary Joe Bryan
3. Gary Joe Bryan

Sandpipers
1. Gary De Cew
2. Robert Mueller

Turnstones
1. Robert Mueller

Plovers
1. Gary Joe Bryan

All Others
1. Gary Joe Bryan
2. Robert Mueller

DECORATIVE SMOOTHIE WADERS
1. Del Herbert
2. Brad Snodgrass
3. Walter Gaskill
HM. Bob Berry
HM. R.D. Wilson

CONTEMPORARY WORKING DECOYS

Best of Contemporary Working Decoys
1. Gary Hanson
2. Steven Cogar
3. Steven Cogar

Puddle Ducks
1. Gary Hanson
2. Steven Cogar
3. Gary Joe Bryan

Wigeon
1. Grant Werdick

All Teal
1. Gary Hanson
2. Steven Cogar
3. Grant Werdick

Wood Duck
1. Gary Joe Bryan

Miscellaneous
1. Steven Cogar

Diving Ducks
1. Anthony Donato
2. Gary Joe Bryan
3. Steven Cogar

Bufflehead
1. Steven Cogar

Goldeneye
1. Ritchey Koch
2. Grant Werdick

Redhead
1. Grant Werdick

Ruddy
1. Gary Joe Bryan

Merganser
1. Brian Moyse
2. Kenneth Crawford

Canvasback
1. Anthony Donato
2. Anthony Donato
3. Anthony Donato

Miscellaneous
1. Steven Cogar

Sea Ducks
1. Grant Werdick
2. Tom and Darlene Westbrock

Sea Ducks
1. Grant Werdick
2. Tom and Darlene Westbrock

Confidence
1. Steven Cogar
2. Gary Joe Bryan
3. Donald Legrand

Confidence
1. Steven Cogar
2. Gary Joe Bryan
3. Donald Legrand
HM. Donald Legrand

SINGLE BRANT
1. Del Herbert
2. Walter Gaskill
3. Joe Girtner

SIX INCH TRADE, HOODED MERGANSER
1. Gary De Cew
2. Joe Girtner
3. Vern Jones
4. Kenneth Crawford
5. Ross Smoker

WILDLIFE AS SCULPTURE
1. Edgar Frank
2. Bill Herbert
3. Bill Herbert

SOON-TO-BE-ANTIQUES

Worn
1. R.D. Wilson
2. R.D. Wilson
3. R.D. Wilson

Pristine
1. R.D. Wilson
2. R.D. Wilson
3. Ross Smoker

Worn (Ducks)
1. R.D. Wilson
2. R.D. Wilson
3. Donald LeGrand

Worn (Geese and Confidence)
1. Karen Hattman

Worn (Shorebirds)
1. R.D. Wilson
2. Ross Smoker
3. Royce Embanks, Jr.

Pristine (Ducks)
1. R.D. Wilson
2. Ross Smoker

Pristine (Shorebirds)
1. R.D. Wilson

Bench
1. Bob Berry
2. Bob Berry
3. Bob Berry
HM. Donald LeGrand

JUNIOR DIVISION
1. Haruki Komeno

SILHOUETTES
1. Del Herbert
2. Hank Wurgler

WILDFOWL HEAD CONTEST
1. Bob Berry
2. Hank Wurgler

WORKING SHOREBIRDS
1. Gary De Cew
2. R.D. Wilson

MINIATURE SONGBIRD
1. R.D. Wilson
2. Hank Wurgler

WILDFOWL HEAD CONTEST
1. Bob Berry
2. Hank Wurgler

MINIATURE SONGBIRD
1. R.D. Wilson
2. Bob Berry
3. Hank Wurgler
4. Everett Rodriguez

SPECIAL CHILDREN'S AWARD
Parker Streit, Photography

Canadian National Wildfowl Carving Championship

BEST OF SHOW
1. Wayne Simkin
2. Pat Godin
3. Jason Lucio

CANADIAN MASTER CLASS

**Decorative Life Size
Floating Ducks**
1. Pat Godin
2. George Mechelse
3. Gary Brocklebank

Working Decoys
1. Dave Ricci
2. George Mechelse

**Life-size Songbirds
with Habitat**
1. Bruce Lepper
2. Bruce Lepper
3. Fred Negrijn

**Birds of Prey and Upland
Game Birds with Habitat**
1. Jim Van Oosten
2. Tom Baldwin

**Waterfowl, Shorebirds,
Seabirds, and Ducks**
1. Wayne Simkin
2. Jason Lucio
3. Jason Lucio
HM. Jason Lucio

**Decorative Miniature
Wildfowl**
1. Jim Van Oosten
2. Fred Negrijn
3. Bob Lavender
HM. Laurie Truehart

OPEN
1. Alex Rios Fernandez
2. Joe Tamborra
3. Jim Edsall

**Decorative Life-size
Floating Ducks**
1. Bruce Mifflin
2. Grant Parks
3. Winston Smith

**Decorative Life-size
Songbirds A**
1. Alex Rios Fernandez
2. Jim Edsall
3. Don Alemany
HM. Uta Strelive
HM. Patrick Chaumand
HM. Don Alemany
HM. Horst Volkman

**Decorative Life-size
Songbirds B**
1. Alex Rios Fernandez
2. Ken Avery
3. Serge Bouchard
HM. Mary Beckstead

Decorative Birds of Prey
1. Winston Smith
2. Serge Bouchard
3. Winston Smith

Decorative Others
1. William Berge
2. Raimo Repo
3. Alex Rios Fernandez

**Decorative Miniature
Wildfowl**
1. Ray Tourangeau
2. Ray Tourangeau
3. Mary Beckstead

**Working and Life-size
Smoothies**
1. Joe Tamborra
2. Bud Frees
3. Bud Frees
HM. Joe Tamborra

INTERMEDIATE
1. Laurie Snelling
2. Robin Deruchie
3. Debra Durfy

**Decorative Life-size
Floating Ducks**
1. Paul Dibranou
2. Ross Scriver
3. Sere Moisan

**Decorative Ducks—
Non-floating**
1. Debra Durfy
2. Peter McLaren
3. Wayne Kristoff

Decorative Songbirds A
1. Lynn Burnett
2. Donald Downey

Decorative Songbirds B
1. Bill Douglas
2. Henry Flaming
3. Ralph Bertrand
HM. Bob Solomon
HM. Wayne Kristoff

Decorative Songbirds C
1. Linda Gawel
2. Wendy Hatch
3. Robin Deruchie
HM. Larry Livingston
HM. Michael Devecchi
HM. Brent Lees

Decorative Birds of Prey
1. Laurie Snelling
2. Laurie Snelling
3. Jay Pollack
HM. Linda Gawel

Decorative Others
1. Bill Douglas
2. Ross Scriver
3. Donald Downey

**Decorative Miniature
Wildfowl**
1. Robin Deruchie
2. Larry Livingston
3. Peter McLaren
HM. Tom Hislop
HM. Tom Hislop

Working Decoys
1. Brent Lees
2. Brent Lees
3. Craig MacLaughlan
HM. Robert Trottier

**Decorative Life-size
Smoothie**
1. Linda Gawel
2. Joe Knauer
HM. Joe Knauer

NOVICE
1. Terry Wilson
2. Morgan Walker
3. Morgan Walker

**Decorative Life-size
Diving Ducks—Floating**
1. T. Wayne Lawson
2. Jeff Earls
3. Barb Scriber

**Decorative Life-size Marsh
Ducks—Floating**
1. Jeff Earls

**Decorative Ducks—
Non-floating**
1. Morgan Walker
2. Morgan Walker
3. John Drewery
HM. Rick Rousseau

Decorative Waterfowl
1. Denise Barletta

Decorative Songbirds A
1. Chris Potter
2. Gary Sitzes
3. Tom Weiler
HM. Sue Pratt

Decorative Songbirds B
1. Allison Laing
2. Sue Priatt
3. Joe Abela

Decorative Songbirds C
1. Joe Abela
2. Denise Barletta

Decorative Birds of Prey
1. Andrew Holmes
2. David Costa
3. Michael Flynn

Decorative Others
1. Laird Beveridge
2. Barb Scriver

**Decorative Miniature
Wildfowl**
1. Roland Crowder
2. Elizabeth Wilson
3. Tom Weiler
HM. Deb Sandilands

**Decorative Life-size
Smoothies**
1. Terry Wilson
2. Denise Barletta

BEGINNER
1. Daryl Chevalier
2. Sierra Eskritt
3. Brian Wooding

**Decorative Ducks
and Waterfowl**
1. Sierra Eskritt
2. Harley Zomer
3. John Ross
HM. Bob Brenzill

**Decorative Life-size
Songbirds**
1. Daryl Chevalier
2. Daryl Chevalier
3. Helen Gray

**Decorative Birds of Prey,
Game Birds, and Shorebirds**
1. Brian Wooding
2. Brian Wooding
3. Daryl Chevalier

Decorative Miniatures
1. Samuel Smallegange

Decorative Others
1. Andrew Flynn

CONTEMPORARY
DECOY CLASS

Expert
1. Ken Hussey
2. Ken Hussey
3. Ken Hussey
HM. Ken Hussey

Amateur
1. John Novak
2. John Novak
3. Nancy Taylor
HM. John Novak

STYLIZED CLASS

Expert
1. Greg Gillespie
2. Alex Rios Fernandez

Amateur
1. Ed Finero
2. Jim Stephen

M&T PRINTING GROUP
PURCHASE AWARD
1. Bruce Lepper
2. George Mechelse
3. Laurie Truehart

ONTARIO DIE COMPANY
PURCHASE AWARD
1. Bruce Lepper
2. Jim Edsall
3. Martin Ward

CHAMPAGNE DUCKS
RUBBERLINE PRODUCTS
LTD. PURCHASE AWARD
1. Jason Lucio
2. Gilles Prud'homme
3. Bob Lavender

MELOCHE PURCHASE
AWARD
1. Greg Gillespie
2. Tom Baldwin
3. Winston Smith

Ohio Decoy Collectors and Carvers Association

IWCA DECORATIVE LIFE-SIZE FLOATING DECOY—OPEN
1. Anthony Donato
2. Pat Godin
3. Pat Godin

Marsh Ducks
1. Anthony Donato
2. Pat Godin
3. Pat Godin

Blue-winged Teal
1. Jack Szolis

Green-winged Teal
1. Gerald Dowling
2. Jack Szolis
3. Jack Szolis

Pintail
1. William Browne

Shoveler
1. Anthony Donato
2. Mike Steed

Wigeon
1. Pat Godin

Wood Duck
1. Pat Godin
2. Cliff Hollestelle

Diving Ducks
1. Ken Stuparyk
2. Mike Steed
3. Warren Brown

Bufflehead
1. Warren Brown
2. Warren Brown

Goldeneye
1. Ken Stuparyk

Ring-necked
1. Mike Steed

Ruddy
1. Jack Szolis

Goose, Confidence, and Sea Ducks
1. Jim Denison
2. Joe Tamborra
3. Mark Swan

Canada Goose
1. Mike Steed

Grebe
1. Joe Tamborra
2. Jack Szolis
3. Jack Szolis

Long-tailed Duck
1. Mark Swan

Loon
1. Jim Denison

Miscellaneous
1. Gerald Dowling
2. Warren Brown
3. Don Fetters

IWCA FLOATING DECORATIVE STYLE DECOY—INTERMEDIATE
1. Ryan Steed
2. Maxine Brown
3. Ryan Steed

Marsh Ducks
1. Robert Bellino
2. Michael Barber
3. Hayden Powell

Wigeon
1. Hayden Powell

Wood Duck
1. Robert Bellino
2. Michael Barber

Diving Ducks
1. Ryan Steed
2. Ryan Steed

Redhead
1. Ryan Steed

Ring-necked
1. Ryan Steed

Goose, Confidence, and Sea Duck
1. Maxine Brown
2. Karen Hattman

Cormorant
1. Karen Hattman

Grebe
1. Maxine Brown

IWCA FLOATING DECORATIVE STYLE DECOY—NOVICE
1. Rick Taylor
2. Karen Mitchell
3. Craig Mitchell

Marsh Ducks
1. Craig Mitchell
2. Rick Mignano
3. Rick Mignano

Green-winged Teal
1. Craig Mitchell

Mallard
1. Rick Mignano
2. Rick Mignano

Diving Ducks
1. Rick Taylor
2. Karen Mitchell
3. Rick Mignano

Bufflehead
1. Jim Spiroff

Canvasback
1. Rick Taylor
2. Rick Mignano
3. Peter Johnson

Ring-necked
1. Karen Mitchell

Scaup
1. Michael Swan

Goose, Confidence, and Sea Ducks
1. Jim Spiroff

Loon
1. Jim Spiroff

REST OF THE MARSH—OPEN
1. Al Jordan
2. Al Jordan
3. Al Jordan

Owl
1. Al Jordan
2. Al Jordan
3. Tom Baldwin

Perching Birds
1. Al Jordan
2. Sandy Czajka
3. Sandy Czajka

Raptors
1. Jim Denison
2. Richard Wells

Upland Game Birds
1. Rod Derdowski
2. Richard Wells
3. Jack Szolis

Miscellaneous
1. Joe Tamborra

REST OF THE MARSH—INTERMEDIATE
1. George Rung
2. George Rung
3. Maxine Brown

Pigeon-like
1. Ted Fisher

Tree-Clinging Birds
1. Maxine Brown
2. George Rung

Shorebirds
1. Ted Fisher
2. Karen Higgins

Miscellaneous
1. George Rung
2. George Rung
3. Karen Higgins

REST OF THE MARSH—NOVICE
1. Ken Harvey
2. Ron Skaggs
3. Paul Bartlett

Tree-clinging Birds
1. Neal Self

Perching Birds
1. Ken Harvey
2. Paul Bartlett
3. Dan Minard

Miscellaneous
1. Ron Skaggs
2. Ron Skaggs
3. Dave Lucht

REST OF THE MARSH MINIATURES—OPEN
1. Gary McNeely
2. Gary McNeely
3. Sandy Czajka

REST OF THE MARSH MINIATURES—INTERMEDIATE
1. Ted Fisher
2. Mitch Myers
3. Mitch Myers

REST OF THE MARSH MINIATURES—NOVICE
1. Neal Self
2. Sandy Wilkins

IWCA-STYLE DECOY—OPEN
1. Pat Godin
2. Pat Godin
3. Pat Godin

Marsh Ducks
1. Pat Godin
2. Pat Godin
3. Tom Christie

Black Duck
1. Michael Wilkins

Blue-winged Teal
1. David Harris
2. Bob Nelson

Cinnamon Teal
1. David Harris

Gadwall
1. Tom Christie

Green-winged Teal
1. Pat Godin
2. David Harris
3. William Beal

Mallard
1. Jim Brace
2. Jim Denison
3. Steve Secord

Pintail
1. Pat Godin
2. Tom Christie
3. Rick Saunders

Shoveler
1. Jack Szolis

Wigeon
1. Jon Jones

Wood Duck
1. Bob Nelson
2. Jim Denison

Diving Ducks
1. Tom Christie
2. Ken Stuparyk
3. Jon Jones

Hooded Merganser
1. Nial Wheeler

Red-breasted Merganser
1. Tom Christie

Ring-necked
1. Ken Stuparyk

Redhead
1. Bud Shell
2. Bruce DiVaccaro
3. Jim Brace

Scaup
1. Jon Jones
2. Jack Szolis

Goose, Confidence, and Sea Duck
1. Pat Godin
2. Gary Joe Bryan
3. Jim Dension

Eider
1. Pat Godin

Grebe
1. Gary Joe Bryan
2. Jim Denison

Harlequin
1. Bud Shell

Long-tailed Duck
1. Nial Wheeler

Cormorant
1. Jack Szolis

IWCA-STYLE DECOY—AMATEUR
1. Vincent Ciola
2. Vincent Ciola
3. Vincent Ciola

Marsh Ducks
1. Vincent Ciola
2. Vincent Ciola
3. Jim Higgins

Black Duck
1. Tom T. Smith
2. Will Turrino

Blue-winged Teal
1. Jim Higgins
2. Darrell Wiggins

Gadwall
1. Vincent Ciola

Green-winged Teal
1. Ron Devuyst

Mallard
1. Don Combs
2. Joe Tarejlas
3. Bob Neal
HM. Tom T. Smith

Pintail
1. Darrel Riggins
2. Paul Bartlett

Shoveler
1. Steven Cogan
2. Tom T. Smith

Wigeon
1. Vincent Ciola

Wood Duck
1. Jim Higgins

Diving Ducks
1. Dean Teigland
2. Steven Cogan
3. Vincent Ciola

Bufflehead
1. Steve Zoller
2. Dean Teigland

Canvasback
1. Dean Teigland
2. Dean Teigland

Goldeneye
1. Steven Cogan

Hooded Merganser
1. Paul Bartlett
2. Antony Donsante
3. Tom T. Smith

Red-breasted Merganser
1. Darrel Riggins
2. Peter Jhmer

Redhead
1. Mike Lodermeier
2. Ted Fisher

Ring-neck
1. Steven Cogan
2. Steven Cogan

Ruddy Duck
1. Paul Bailey
2. Ted Fisher
3. Tom T. Smith

Scaup
1. Vincent Ciola
2. Michael Frechette
3. Vincent Lori
HM. Don Combs
HM. Don Combs
HM. Garrett Secord

Goose, Confidence, and Sea Duck
1. Vincent Ciola
2. Michael Frechette
3. Michael Frechette

Canada Goose
1. Vincent Ciola

Eider
1. Peter Jhmer

Grebe
1. Tom T. Smith

Razorbill
1. Michael Frechette

Harlequin
1. Mark Langenderfer

Scoter
1. Michael Frechette
2. Peter Jhmer

IWCA-STYLE DECOY—
JUNIOR
1. Logan Brewer
2. Stephen White
3. Garret Brewer

Wood Duck
1. Garret Brewer

Canvasback
1. Andrew Lewis

Scaup
1. Logan Brewer
2. Stephen White

Bufflehead
1. Jason Brewer

IWCA-STYLE SHOREBIRD
DECOY CHAMPIONSHIP
1. Bruce DiVaccaro
2. Bruce DiVaccaro
3. Tod Van Wieren

Curlew, Godwit, Whimbrel
1. Bruce DiVaccaro
2. Tod Van Wieren

Willets, Yellowlegs
1. Andy Chlupsa

Plovers
1. Gary Joe Bryan

Sandpipers, Dunlins
1. Bruce DiVaccaro
2. Tod Van Wieren
3. Jack Szolis

**Turnstones, Knots, and
Dowitchers**
1. Jack Szolis

Avocets, Stilts
1. Jim Denison
2. Jim Dension
3. Gayle Crouch

Wading Birds
1. Tom Baldwin
2. Gary Joe Bryan

Other Shorebirds
1. Gary Joe Bryan
2. Andy Chlupsa
3. Gary Joe Bryan

IWCA-STYLE SHOREBIRD—
OPEN
1. Bruce DiVaccaro
2. Andy Chlupsa
3. Gary Joe Bryan

Willets, Yellowlegs
1. Andy Chlupsa

Plovers
1. Gary Joe Bryan

Sandpipers, Dunlins
1. Bruce DiVaccaro
2. Tod Van Wieren
3. Jim Brace

Avocets, Stilts
1. Gayle Crouch

Wading Birds
1. Gary Joe Bryan

Other
1. Andy Chlupsa
2. Gary Joe Bryan

IWCA-STYLE SHOREBIRD—
AMATEUR
1. Mark Prinster
2. Steve Stamberry
3. George Keller

Killdeer
1. George Keller
2. Dennis Roberts
3. Mark Langenderfer

Sandpipers, Dunlins
1. Steve Stamberry
2. Dennis Roberts
3. John Mawer

Avocets, Stilts
1. Michael Swan
2. Mark Langenderfer

Plovers
1. Mark Prinster

Other
1. Ted Fisher

WORKING SHOREBIRD
DECOY AND SILHOUETTE
1. Bruce DiVaccaro
2. Gary Joe Bryan
3. Garret Secord

WILDFOWLERS SINGLE
DECOY
1. Ken Stuparyk
2. Gary Hanson
3. George Keller

Marsh Ducks
1. Gary Hanson
2. Tom Matus
3. George Keller

Black Duck
1. Peter Rivicki
2. Brian Moyse
3. Joe Brewer

Blue-winged Teal
1. Scott Green
2. Tom Wood
3. Daniel Wise

Cinnamon Teal
1. Grant Weddick

Gadwall
1. Jim Higgins
2. George Williams

Green-winged Teal
1. Dave Speer
2. Daniel Green

Mallard
1. George Keller
2. Tom Matus
3. George Keller
HM. Gary Hanson

Pintail
1. Tom Matus
2. Tom Matus
3. Jason Chaley

Shoveler
1. Matt Brooks
2. Jason Chaley

Wigeon
1. Gary Hanson
2. Steven Cogar
3. Ron Kurkowski
HM. Tom Matus
HM. Tom Matus
HM. Andy Pope

Wood Duck
1. Dan Appel
2. Duane Ganser
3. John Nelson

Miscellaneous
1. Jason Chaley
2. Jason Chaley
3. Gary Joe Bryan

Diving Ducks
1. Ken Stuparyk
2. George Keller
3. Gary Hanson

Barrow's Goldeneye
1. Corey Green
2. Tod Van Wieren
3. Dave Regnier
HM. Tod Van Wieren

Bufflehead
1. Brian Moyse
2. Gary Joe Bryan
3. Brian Moyse
HM. Brian Moyse

Canvasback
1. Peter Rivicki
2. Tom Rowe
3. Tom Rowe

Common Goldeneye
1. Ken Stuparyk
2. Tom Matus
3. Craig Smith
HM. Jim Allor
HM. Brian Moyse
HM. Brian Moyse
HM. Ron Kurkowski
HM. George Keller

Hooded Merganser
1. George Keller
2. Ken Stuparyk
3. Aaron Condon
HM. Steven Cogar
HM. Brian Moyse

Common Merganser
1. Gary Hanson
2. Danny Lewis

Red-breasted Merganser
1. Pat Pietroski

Redhead
1. Tom Matus
2. Tom Matus
3. Grant Weddick
HM. Mike Ludermeirer
HM. Daniel Greene

Ring-necked
1. Ron Kurkoswki
2. Jim Allor
3. Daniel Wise

Ruddy Duck
1. Gary Joe Bryan
2. Scott Green
3. Tyler Frank
HM. Andy Hildreth
HM. Andy Hildreth

Scaup
1. Tom Rowe
2. Tom Rowe
3. Brian Moyse
HM. Scott Irwin
HM. Brian Moyse

*Goose, Confidence, and Sea
Ducks*
1. Gary Hanson
2. Brian Moyse
3. Gary Joe Bryan

Brant
1. Scott Green
2. George Williams

Canada Goose
1. Tom Matus
2. Steven Cogar

Common Scoter
1. Peter Rivicki

Coot
1. Tom Wood
2. Grant Weddick

Grebe
1. Gary Joe Bryan
2. Gary Joe Bryan
3. Tom Wood

King Eider
1. Russell Owen
2. Tim Bombardier

Long-tailed
1. Gary Hanson
2. Robert Coats

Scoter
1. Peter Johnson
2. Walt Papke
3. Brian Moyse

Miscellaneous Goose
1. Tom Matus
2. Scott Green

Miscellaneous Sea Duck
1. Brian Moyse
2. Brian Moyse
3. Grant Weddick

WILDFOWLERS SHOOTING
STOOL SIX BIRD RIG

Marsh Ducks, Open
1. Luke Costilow
2. George Williams
3. Matt Brooks

Divers, Open
1. Gary Hanson
2. Jeff Galat
3. Dave Regnier

*Goose, Confidence, Sea
Ducks*
1. Aaron Condon

SPECIAL CONTEST LADIES
DAY IN THE POOL--
DABBLERS

*Sponsored by the Duck
Blind*
1. Glenn Sweet
2. Jim Higgins
3. Steven Cogar

JUNIOR WATERFOWLERS

Ages 9 and younger
1. Colton Johnson
2. Jaxson Brewer
3. Vijay Dezeuw
HM. Michael Pieth
HM. Brian Smar

JUNIOR WATERFOWLERS

Ages 10–13
1. Jack Pietch

JUNIOR WATERFOWLERS

Ages 14–17
1. Garrett Brewer
2. Jayvin Roush
3. David Pilarski

IT AIN'T VINTAGE YET
1. Ken Hussey
2. Ken Hussey
3. Scott Green

Ducks
1. Ken Hussey
2. Scott Green
3. Ken Hussey
HM. Dean Teigland

Shorebirds
1. Al Cretney
2. Ken Yacavone

Confidence
1. Ken Hussey
2. Ken Hussey
3. Herb Falkinburg

DOVE CONTEST
1. Andy Chlupsa
2. Brad Falkinburg
3. Ken Yacavone

SHOREBIRD CARVE AT
HOME AND PAINT AT
SHOW
1. Brad Falkinburg
2. Andy Chlupsa
3. Garrett Secord

DECOY PAINT AT SHOW

Bluebill—Open
1. Gary Hanson
2. Jim Brace
3. David Harris

Bluebill—Junior
1. Abby Clark
HM. Sarah Clayton
HM. Peter Johnson

COCKTAIL BIRD
1. Gary Doviak
2. Jim Denison
3. Brad Falkinburg

WARD WORLD YOUTH
SILHOUETTE CONTEST
1. Ethan Falkinburg
2. Josh Hartwell
3. Daniel Tomalak

FLAT ART
1. Tim Taylor
2. Jocelyn Beatty
3. Matt Clayton
HM. Pat Costilow

OHIO FEDERAL JUNIOR
DUCK STAMP
1. Karen Sung

Pacific Brant Carving and Art Show

SPECIAL AWARDS
PEOPLE'S CHOICE
Rick Zuchetto

CARVER'S CHOICE
Jai Kealy
Bob Lavender

BEST BRANT
1. Vern Jones
2. Vern Jones

BEST HUNTING DECOY
Harvey Welch

BEST ENDANGERED
SPECIES (BURROWING
OWL)
Novice: Wayne MacDonald
Advanced: Randy Joy
Expert: Sharon Hubbard

BEST ANTIQUE-STYLE
DECOY
Ducks: Roy Koyama
Shorebirds: Bill Beese
Geese: Sharon Hubbard

CABELA'S CANADA
AWARDS
Green-wing Teal Drake:
Malcolm Ho-you
Spruce Grouse: Jack Tucker
Least Sandpiper: Barry Saunders

BEST COCKTAIL CLASS
Air
1. Bob Lavender
2. Harold Last
3. Rob Swanton
HM. Leroy Royer
Land
1. Malcolm Ho-You
Water
1. Diane Craven
2. Dennis Drechsler
3. Wayne MacDonald

EXPERT
1. Bob Lavender
Realistic Life-size Waterbirds
1. Austin Eade
2. Vern Jones
3. Vern Jones
Marsh Ducks
1. Malcolm Ho-You
2. Malcolm Ho-You
3. Barry Saunders

Diving Ducks
1. Austin Eade
Geese, Swans
1. Vern Jones
2. Vern Jones
3. Dan Vukicevic
Seabirds, Shorebirds, Others
1. Harvey Welch
Realistic Life-size Landbirds
1. Bob Lavender
2. Bob Lavender
Small Songbirds
1. Bob Lavender
Large Songbirds
1. Bob Lavender
2. Harvey Welch
3. Dieter Golze
Upland Gamebirds
1. Vern Jones
2. Barry Saunders
Raptors
1. Bob Lavender
2. Malcolm Ho-You
3. Ted Jarvis
Realistic Miniature Birds
1. Dieter Golze
2. Harvey Welch
3. Bob Lavender
Waterbirds
1. Bob Lavender
2. Bill Beese
Landbirds
1. Dieter Golze
2. Harvey Welch
3. Bob Lavender
Hunting Decoys
1. Harvey Welch
2. Vern Jones
Diving Ducks
1. Harvey Welch
Geese, Swans, Confidence
1. Vern Jones
Contemporary Decoys—Non-floating
1. Vern Jones
2. Malcolm Ho-You
3. Vern Jones
Marsh and Diving Ducks
1. Malcolm Ho-You
2. Vern Jones
3. Vern Jones
Geese, Swans, and Confidence
1. Vern Jones
2. Harvey Welch

Antique-style Decoys
1. Roy Koyama
2. Bill Beese
3. Sharon Hubbard
Ducks
1. Roy Koyama
Geese, Swans, and Confidence
1. Sharon Hubbard
Shorebirds
1. Bill Beese
2. Sharon Hubbard

ADVANCED
1. Rob Gander
Realistic Life-size Waterbirds
1. Ken Vickets
Marsh Ducks
1. John Burwash
2. Bruce Walker
Diving Ducks
1. Ken Vickets
2. Bruce Walker
3. Bruce Walker
Geese and Swans
1. D.B. (Dan) Young
Seabirds, Shorebirds, and Others
1. Vern Black
Realistic Life-size Landbirds
1. Bruce Walker
Small Songbirds
1. Randy Joy
2. John Burwash
3. Francoise Guilbault
Medium Songbirds
1. Diane Craven
2. K. Louise Smith
3. Wayne Myers
Large Songbirds
1. Randy Joy
2. Ernie Fehr
3. Wayne Myers
HM. Harold Last
Raptors
1. Bruce Walker
2. Randy Joy
3. Francoise Guilbault
Others
1. Margaret Beswetherick
Realistic Miniature Birds
1. Dennis Drechsler

Waterbirds
1. Dennis Drechsler
2. Leroy Royer
3. Vern Black
Landbirds
1. Jack Tucker
2. Wayne Myers
3. Vern Black
Hunting Decoys
1. Leroy Royer
Contemporary Decoys—Non-floating
1. Alan K. Spiller
Marsh & Diving Ducks
1. Alan K. Spiller
Shorebirds
1. Joany Hughes-Games
Antique-style Decoys
1. Ken Vickets
2. Rob Swanton
3. Ken Vickets
Interpretive/Stylized
1. Robert Gander
2. John Burwash
3. John Burwash
3. Barry Bell

INTERMEDIATE
1. Jim Price
Realistic Life-size Waterbirds
1. Jim Price
2. Annette MacDonald
Realistic Life-size Landbirds
1. Rick Zuchetto
Small Songbirds
1. Rick Zuchetto
2. Betty Erb
Medium Songbirds
1. Rick Zuchetto
2. Jim Price
3. Peter Dueck
Large Songbirds
1. Peter Dueck
Upland Gamebirds
1. Ed Shaske
Raptors
1. Ed Schaske
2. Ed Schaske
Realistic Miniature Birds
1. Annette MacDonald

NOVICE
1. Wayne MacDonald
Realistic Life-size Waterbirds
1. Dave Macfie

Marsh Ducks
1. Norman Rothwell
2. Wayne MacDonald
3. Thomas McColm
Diving Ducks
1. Cliff Suntjens
Seabirds, Shorebirds, and Others
1. Dave Macfie
2. Keith Baker
3. Keith Baker
Realistic Life-size Landbirds
1. Wayne MacDonald
Small Songbirds
1. Simone Chenier
2. Thomas McColm
3. Thomas McColm
Medium Songbirds
1. Norman Rothwell
2. Keith Baker
3. Dave Taylor
HM. Keith Baker
HM. Jim Turney
Large Songbirds
1. Thomas McColm
2. Thomas McColm
3. Keith Baker
Raptors
1. Wayne MacDonald
2. Norman Rothwell
3. Dave Macfie
Realistic Miniature Birds
1. Mike Scott
Waterbirds
1. Keith Baker
Landbirds
1. Mike Scott
2. Dave Taylor
Hunting Decoys
1. Dave Macfie
Interpretive/Stylized
1. Marcella O'Black
2. Kerry Davis
3. Gail Laug

YOUTH
1. Dyson Blitterswyk
Age 11 and under
1. Sophia Labonte
Age 12 through 14
1. Dyson Blitterswyk
2. Savanna Labonte
Age 15 through 18
1. Lin Zhuolin Wu
2. Lin Zhuolin Wu

Pacific Flyway Decoy Classic

OPEN DECORATIVE LIFE-
SIZE FLOATING
1. Anthony Donato
2. Leonard Rousseau
3. Terry Avila

Dabbling Ducks
1. Leonard Rousseau
2. Terry Avila
3. Brad Snodgrass

Wigeon
1. Brad Snodgrass
2. Craig Mortimore

Green-winged Teal
1. Leonard Rousseau
2. Terry Avila
3. Gerald Dowling

Cinnamon Teal
1. Brad Snodgrass

Other Dabblers
1. Anthony Donato
2. Gerald Dowling

Geese/Brant
1. Anthony Donato

PFDA HUNTING DECOYS
1. Del Herbert
2. Andy White
3. Andy White

Dabbling Ducks

Pintail
1. Chet Wilcox
2. Chuck Peterson

Wigeon
1. Laurie Fausett

Shoveler
1. Chet Wilcox

Green-winged Teal
1. Ross Smoker
2. Wade Kelly
3. Anthony Donato

Cinnamon Teal
1. Chet Wilcox

Other Dabblers
1. Andy White

Diving Ducks
1. Roger Anderson
2. Chet Wilcox
3. Lloyd Heins

Canvasback
1. Roger Anderson
2. Lloyd Heins
3. Ciro Juarez

Bufflehead
1. Chet Wilcox

Ruddy Duck
1. Jim Donaldson

Other Divers
1. Jim Donaldson

Geese
1. Del Herbert
2. Michael Peters
3. Michael Peters

Brant
1. Lloyd Heins
2. Michael Peters
3. Laurie Fausett
HM. Tom Matus

All Confidence
1. Andy White
2. Ross Smoker
3. Andy White

CONTEMPORARY DECOYS
1. Tom Christie
2. Jon Jones
3. Tom Christie

Dabbling Ducks
1. Tom Christie
2. Tom Christie
3. Tom Christie

Wigeon
1. Peter Reding

Gadwall
1. Tom Christie
2. Tom Christie
3. Leonard Rousseau

Shoveler
1. Andy White

Green-winged Teal
1. Chet Wilcox
2. Peter Reding

Other Dabblers
1. Tom Matus

Diving Ducks
1. Jon Jones
2. Craig Mortimore
3. Chris Nicolai

Scaup
1. Craig Mortimore

Scoters
1. Chris Nicolai

Long-tailed Duck
1. Jon Jones

All Geese
1. Tom Matus
2. Wade Kelly

FIELD OR STICK-UP
DECOYS
1. Gary De Cew
2. Gary De Cew
3. Jim Burcio
HM. Jim Donaldson
HM. Jim Burcio

WALL HANGERS
1. Bob Berry
2. Tony Percolatto
3. R.D. Wilson

DECORATIVE LIFE-SIZE
WILDFOWL
1. Brock Hinton
2. Craig Mortimore
3. Bob Berry

Waterfowl
1. Brock Hinton
2. James Marieiro

Upland Game
1. Larry Woods
2. Chet Wilcox
3. Chet Wilcox

Shorebirds/Waders
1. Bob Berry
2. Gary Smoot
3. Chet Wilcox
HM. Chet Wilcox

Raptors
1. Gary Smoot
2. Dick Marshall
3. Chet Wilcox
HM. Chet Wilcox

Songbirds
1. Craig Mortimore
2. Chet Wilcox
3. Lynda Goff
HM. Chet Wilcox
HM. Chet Wilcox

DECORATIVE MINIATURE
WILDFOWL
1. Gerald Painter
2. Craig Mortimore
3. Gary De Cew

Waterfowl
1. Peter Reding

Upland Game
1. Gerald Painter

Shorebirds/Waders
1. Gary De Cew

Songbirds
1. Craig Mortimore

BOB PETERSEN GUNNING
SHOREBIRDS
1. Peter Palumbo
2. Tommy Stewart
3. Tommy Stewart

*Curlews, Godwits,
Whimbrels*
1. Chet Wilcox

Willets, Yellowlegs
1. Peter Palumbo
2. Tommy Stewart
3. Chet Wilcox
HM. Chet Wilcox

Sandpipers, Dunlins
1. Tommy Stewart
2. Del Herbert
3. Chet Wilcox
HM. Dick Marshall
HM. Chet Wilcox

Plovers
1. Chet Wilcox
2. Brad Snodgrass
3. Chet Wilcox

*Turnstones, Knots,
Dowitchers*
1. Jim Burcio
2. Del Herbert
3. Chet Wilcox
HM. Chet Wilcox

Avocets, Stilts
1. Del Herbert
2. Chet Wilcox

All Other Shorebirds
1. Andy White
2. Craig Mortimore

CALIFORNIA RICE
COMMISSION—
AMERICAN AVOCET
1. Gary De Cew
2. Andy White
3. Jim Burcio
HM. Del Herbert

CALIFORNIA RICE
COMMISSION— DRAKE
REDHEAD
1. Walter Gaskill
2. Andy White
3. Wade Kelly
HM. Roger Anderson
HM. Don Hovie

C.W.A. CARVER OF THE
YEAR—DRAKE REDHEAD
1. Walter Gaskill
2. Del Herbert
3. Terry Avila
HM. Roger Anderson
HM. Tom Matus
HM. Anthony Donato

THREE-BIRD RIG
1. Roger Anderson
2. Tom Matus
3. Joe Freitas
HM. Lance Hebdon
HM. Chet Wilcox

DOUBTFUL ANTIQUES
1. R.D. Wilson
2. R.D. Wilson
3. Dick Marshall

Ducks
1. R.D. Wilson
2. Laurie Fausett
3. Dick Marshall
HM. R.D. Wilson
HM. Laurie Fausett
HM. Dick Marshall
HM. Laurie Fausett

Shorebirds
1. R.D. Wilson
2. R.D. Wilson
3. Dick Marshall
HM. Dick Marshall
HM. Donald Dunlap
HM. Donald Dunlap
HM. Donald Dunlap

Goose/Confidence
1. R.D. Wilson
2. Dick Marshall
3. Jim Burcio
HM. Ross Smoker

MINIATURE DECOY—
DRAKE WOOD DUCK
1. Jerry Harris
2. Don Hovie
3. Brad Snodgrass

U.S. FISH AND WILDLIFE—
CALIFORNIA CONDOR
1. Gary Smoot

U.S. FISH AND WILDLIFE—
MALE CALIFORNIA QUAIL
1. Don Hovie
2. Chet Wilcox

CLASSIC SWAP DECOY—
DRAKE WOOD DUCK
1. Joe Girtner
2. Jerry Harris
3. Bob Joseph
HM. Ken Nelson

FEATHERWEIGHT
DECOYS—DRAKE BLUE-
WINGED TEAL
1. Tom Matus
2. Gary De Cew
3. Rob Capriola

UMAGOOLIE
1. R.D. Wilson
2. Brad Snodgrass
3. Bill Peters
HM. Joe Green
HM. Gary Smoot

SEA DUCKS/
MERGANSERS—
SPECTACLED EIDER
1. Walter Gaskill

INTERNATIONAL
WILDFOWL
1. Walter Gaskill
2. Brad Snodgrass
3. Don Hovie

INTERMEDIATE
DECORATIVE LIFE-SIZE
FLOATING
1. Jim Donaldson
2. Rick Pass
3. Chuck Engberg

Dabblers
1. Chuck Engberg
2. Rick Pass
3. Rick Pass

Pintail
1. Rick Pass
2. Chuck Engberg

Wigeon
1. Chuck Engberg

Green-winged Teal
1. Rick Pass

Cinnamon Teal
1. Rick Pass

Wood Duck
1. Chuck Engberg

Diving Ducks
1. Rick Pass
2. Rick Pass
3. Rick Pass

Canvasback
1. Rick Pass

Bufflehead
1. Rick Pass
2. Chuck Engberg

Ruddy Duck
1. Chuck Engberg

Merganser
1. Rick Pass

Geese and Confidence

All Confidence
1. Jim Donaldson

CONTEMPORARY DECOYS

Dabbling Ducks
1. Jim Higgins
2. Jim Higgins

DECORATIVE LIFE-SIZE WILDFOWL
1. Jim Donaldson
2. Rick Pass
3. Chuck Engberg

Waterfowl
1. Jim Donaldson

Upland Game
1. Hank Wurgler
2. Jim Donaldson
3. Jim Donaldson

Shorebirds/Waders
1. Hank Wurgler
2. Jim Donaldson
3. Hank Wurgler
HM. Thomas Oakes

Raptors
1. Hank Wurgler

Songbirds
1. Hank Wurgler
2. Hank Wurgler
3. Hank Wurgler
HM. Hank Wurgler
HM. Hank Wurgler

DECORATIVE MINIATURE WILDFOWL
1. Hank Wurgler
2. Hank Wurgler
3. Hank Wurgler

Upland Game
1. Hank Wurgler
2. Hank Wurgler

Shorebirds/Waders
1. Hank Wurgler

Songbirds
1. Hank Wurgler
2. Hank Wurgler

NOVICE DECORATIVE LIFESIZE WILDFOWL
1. Dave Paul
2. Dave Paul
3. Dave Paul

Waterfowl
1. Dave Paul
2. Dave Paul

Upland Game
1. Ron Krug
2. David Moore

Seabirds
1. Bill Peters

Raptors
1. Dave Paul
2. John Hannebolton
3. John Finlay

Songbirds
1. Dave Paul
2. Dave Paul
3. John Hannebolton
HM. John Hannebolton
HM. Vickie Lee Karabinis

PFDA HUNTING DECOYS
1. Tim Murphy
2. Danny Lewis
3. Ken Nelson

Dabbling Ducks
1. Tim Murphy
2. Ken Nelson
3. Danny Lewis

Mallards
1. Tim Murphy
2. Ken Nelson
3. Bill Peters
HM. Bill Peters
HM. Vickie Lee Karabinis
HM. Ken Nelson

Green-wing Teal
1. Ken Nelson

Other Dabblers
1. Danny Lewis

Diving Ducks
1. Danny Lewis
2. Danny Lewis

Scaup
1. Danny Lewis

Eider
1. Danny Lewis

Goose and Confidence
1. Danny Lewis
2. Bill Peters
3. Bill Peters

DECORATIVE MINIATURE WILDFOWL
1. Dave Paul
2. Bill Peters
3. Bill Peters
HM. Bill Peters

Waterfowl
1. Dave Paul
2. Bill Peters
3. Bill Peters

BENCH CLASS
1. Bret Hicks
2. Rick Pass
3. Bret Hicks
HM. Dave Paul
HM. Vickie Lee Karabinis

JUNIOR CARVER (0–14 YEARS)
1. Jonus Kobylik
2. Katie Hanberry
3. Erik Van Steinburg
HM. Liam Hanberry

JUNIOR CARVER (15-17 YEARS)
1. Allen Kobylik

DICK AND JINX TROON AWARD
1. Anthony Donato

JINX TROON PAINTING CONTEST
1. Peter Palumbo
2. Rob Capriola
3. Jim Burcio
HM. Dick Marshall

Ward World Championship

WORLD

Decorative Life-size Wildfowl
1. Gary Eigenberger, Green Bay, WI
2. Joshua Guge, Pingree Grove, IL
3. Alan Jordan, Rochester, NY

Decorative Life-size Waterfowl Pair
1. Larry Fell, Belleville, CA
2. Rick Bobincheck, McClellandtown, PA
3. Anthony Donato, Fresno, CA

Decorative Miniature Wildfowl
1. Gerald Painter, Great Falls, MT
2. Gary Eigenberger, Green Bay, WI
3. Jeff Krete, Cambridge, ON

Interpretive Wood Sculpture
1. Lynn Branson, Courtenay, BC
2. Tom Baldwin, Cuyahoga Falls, OH
3. Daniel Montano, Spring Valley, CA

Shootin' Rig
1. Keith Mueller, Killingworth, CT
2. Thomas Flemming, Minnetrista, MN
3. Tom Christie, Waverly, IA

MASTERS

Decorative Life-size Floating Waterfowl
1. Kent Duff
2. Pat Godin
3. Doug Mason

Marsh Ducks
1. Pat Godin
2. Doug Mason
3. Al Fulford

Diving Ducks
1. David Van Lanen
2. Glenn McMurdo
3. Daniel Montano

Decorative Life-size Wildfowl
1. Gary Eigenberger
2. Gerald Painter
3. J. Richard Finch

Waterfowl, Shorebirds, Wading Birds, and Seabirds
1. Billy Crockett, III
2. Glenn McMurdo
3. Robert Kroese

Upland Game Birds and Birds of Prey
1. Gary Eigenberger
2. J. Richard Finch
3. Alan Jordan

Land Birds and Songbirds
1. Gerald Painter
2. Thomas Horn
3. Gary Yoder

Decorative Miniature Wildfowl
1. Gary Eigenberger
2. Gary Eigenberger
3. Gary Eigenberger

Interpretive Wood Sculpture
1. Gary Eigenberger
2. Bill Casto
3. Bill Casto

ADVANCED

Decorative Life-size Floating Waterfowl
1. Joe Tamorra
2. Joe Tamorra
3. Theodore Smith

Marsh Ducks
1. Anthony Donato
2. George Mechelse
3. Glenn Lofton

Black Duck
1. Gregory Taylor
2. Gary Gentilcore

Blue-winged Teal
1. Peter Downes
2. Don Gabelhouse
3. Lon Bernth

Gadwall
1. Clark Weaver
2. Fred Miller
3. Anthony Licciardello

Green-winged Teal
1. Leonard Rousseau
2. John Butterfield

Northern Pintail
1. George Mechelse
2. Richard Quillen

Shoveler
1. Anthony Donato

Wigeon
1. Vern Jones
2. Raymond Hann

Wood Duck
1. Glenn Lofton
2. Fred Miller
3. Lon Bernth

All Other
1. Guy Rouleau

Diving Ducks
1. Joe Tamorra
2. Peter Downes
3. Grant Parks

Bufflehead
1. Warren Brown
2. Warren Brown
3. Edward Clark, Jr.

Canvasback
1. Peter Downes
2. Benoit Therrien
3. John Butterfield

Common Merganser
1. Brent Thomas

Eider
1. Guy Rouleau

Hooded Merganser
1. Joe Tamorra
2. Randolph Hansen
3. Gary Brocklebank

Red-breasted Merganser
1. Grant Parks
2. Henry Stoehr
3. Russ Clark

Redhead
1. Benoit Therrien
2. Tom Scanlan

Ring-necked Duck
1. Glenn Lofton
2. Raymond Hann

Ruddy Duck
1. Don Gabelhouse

Scaup
1. Leonard Rousseau
2. John Cardello
3. Robert Duclos

Scoter
1. John Butterfield

Geese, Swan, and Confidence
1. Joe Tamorra
2. Theodore Smith
3. Guy St. Arnaud

Brant
1. Jean Lalonde

Canada Goose
1. Norman Wise

Coot
1. Hank Sprouse

Grebe
1. Joe Tamorra
2. Theodore Smith
3. Guy St. Arnaud

Loon
1. Dick Zechmann

All Other Geese
1. George Wickham

Decorative Life-size Wildfowl
1. Greg Pedersen
2. Alex Rios
3. Jerry Simchuk

Waterfowl
1. Ben Benedict
2. Lon Bernth
3. Vern Jones

Shorebirds and Wading Birds
1. Jim Edsall
2. Randolph Hansen
3. Yasuyuki Nemoto

Upland Game Birds
1. Daniel Ross
2. Randolph Hansen
3. Richard Quillen
HM. Richard Rossiter
HM. Richard Quillen

Birds of Prey
1. Jim Van Oosten
2. William Kempen
3. Ronnie Zint
HM. William Kempen
HM. Jennifer Felton
HM. Laurie Truehart
HM. Kenneth Alvey
HM. Richard Rossiter
HM. Kenneth Alvey

Songbirds A
1. Greg Pedersen
2. Jerry Simchuk
3. Alex Rios
HM. Greg Pedersen
HM. Jim Edsall
HM. Jim Edsall

Songbirds B
1. Alex Rios
2. Dennis Gorczany
3. Kathryn Hritz
HM. Vicky Theis
HM. Clark Weaver

Non-passerine Land Birds
1. Patrick Chaumard
2. Brian Sandwich
3. Alex Rios
HM. Atsuko Umekawa
HM. Toshiaki Yamasaki
HM. Rene Eugenio

Decorative Miniature Wildfowl
1. Pat Moore
2. Greg Pedersen
3. Alex Rios

Waterfowl
1. Raymond Tourangeau
2. William Beese
3. Ben Benedict

Shorebirds and Wading Birds
1. William Beese
2. Jim Edsall
3. Kathy Marchut
HM. Gary De Cew

Upland Game Birds
1. Pat Moore
2. Atsuko Umekawa
3. Bob Hand, Jr.
HM. Raymond Tourangeau

Birds of Prey
1. Jim Van Oosten
2. Ronnie Zint
3. Norman Wise
HM. Ted Stewart

Songbirds A
1. Greg Pedersen
2. Tom Baldwin
3. Richard Snyder
HM. Richard Snyder

Songbirds B
1. Randy Connor
2. Richard Snyder

Non-passerine Land Birds
1. Alex Rios
2. William Beese
3. Richard Snyder

Interpretive Wood Sculpture
1. William Cott
2. Claire Williams
3. Tom Scanlan
HM. Larry Hare
HM. Alex Rios

INTERMEDIATE

Best in Show
1. Bruce Mifflin
2. Richard Clark
3. Deborah Garman

Decorative Life-size Floating
1. Bruce Mifflin
2. Richard Clark
3. Deborah Garman

Marsh Ducks
1. Richard Clark
2. Donald Huber
3. Dan Meloche

Black Duck
1. Richard Clark

Blue-winged Teal
1. Richard Clark
2. Donald Huber
3. Robert Murray
HM. Don Miller

Green-winged Teal
1. E.J. Felarise
2. E.J. Felarise
3. Dwinton Morgan
HM. Andrew Speer

Mallard
1. Dan Meloche
2. Dwinton Morgan

Shoveler
1. Philip Willey

Wood Duck
1. Robert Bellino

All Other
1. Donald Huber

Diving Ducks
1. Bruce Mifflin
2. Richard Clark
3. Deborah Garman

Bufflehead
1. Richard Clark
2. Austin Eade

Canvasback
1. Dwinton Morgan
2. Robert Jones
3. Robert Jones
HM. Ronald Bevins

Common Merganser
1. Robert Bellion

Eider
1. Eric Megargel
2. Craig Boyhont

Goldeneye
1. Richard Clark
2. Wayne Kidd

Hooded Merganser
1. Bruce Mifflin
2. Deborah Garman
3. Brad Kelly

Long-tailed Duck
1. Bud Seymour

Red-breasted Merganser
1. Richard Clark

Redhead
1. Rodney Lee

Ruddy Duck
1. Donald Guilbault

Scaup
1. Zenon Gawel

All Other
1. John Ness

Geese, Swans, and Confidence
1. Donald Guilbault
2. Maxine Brown
3. Andrew Speer

Grebe
1. Donald Guilbault
2. Maxine Brown
3. Andrew Speer

Decorative Life-size Wildfowl
1. Karen Hess
2. Horst Volkmann
3. Jeannine Audet

Waterfowl
1. Jeannine Audet
2. Toni Kayson
3. Daniel Irons
HM Edward Svoboda
HM. Donald McHugh

Shorebirds and Wading Birds
1. Tom Jones
2. Takeuchi Misako
3. Robert Gray
HM. Karen Hattman
HM. Timothy Curley

Seabirds
1. Paul Knight
2. Douglas Mar

Upland Game Birds
1. Harold Stalker
2. Bruce Munro

Birds of Prey
1. Karen Hess
2. Vern Hesketh
3. Art Wolff
HM. Vern Hesketh
HM. Reuben Unger
HM. Mark Madden

Songbirds A
1. Horst Volkmann
2. James Cummings
3. Toni Kayson
HM. Laurie Snelling

Songbirds B
1. Austin Eade
2. Wendy Hatch
3. Vern Hesketh
HM. Vern Hesketh
HM. Mark Langford

Non-passerine Land Birds
1. Vern Hesketh
2. Isaac Laboy
3. Toni Kayson
HM. Maxine Brown

Decorative Miniature Wildfowl
1. Reuben Unger
2. Robert Kelley
3. Robert Orr

Waterfowl
1. Butch Slaughter
2. Robin Deruchie
3. Rodney Lee

Shorebirds and Wading Birds
1. Robert Kelley
2. Butch Slaughter
3. John Crowell
HM. Janice Doppler
HM. John Crowell

Seabirds
1. Robert Kelley

Upland Game Birds
1. Robert Kelley

Birds of Prey
1. Reuben Unger
2. Mark Madden
3. Dave Weatherbee
HM. Timothy Curley

Songbirds A
1. Robert Orr

Songbirds B
1. Dave Weatherbee

Interpretive Wood Sculpture
1. Pamela Wilson
2. Donald McHugh
3. Robert Plitko
HM. Isaac Laboy
HM. Bruce Munro
HM. Donald McHugh
HM. Isaac Laboy
HM. Isaac Laboy

Bench
1. Laurie Snelling
2. Mary Beckstead
3. Mark Madden

NOVICE
1. Michael Jackson
2. Leonel Gonzales
3. Leonel Gonzales

Decorative Life-size Floating Waterfowl
1. Michael Jackson
2. Robert Strachan
3. David Gutbrod

Marsh Ducks
1. David Gutbrod
2. David Gutbrod
3. Rick Pass

Blue-winged Teal
1. Scott Lebakken
2. Mark Fontenot

Green-winged Teal
1. David Gutbrod
2. Rick Pass
3. Tim Hipple
HM. Harold Brown
HM. Rick Pass

Northern Pintail
1. Rick Pass

Wigeon
1. David Gutbrod

Wood Duck
1. Ronald Fleischer

Diving Ducks
1. Robert Strachan
2. David Jayne
3. Rick Pass

Bufflehead
1. David Jayne
2. James Kimble
3. Rick Pass
HM. Harold Brown

Canvasback
1. Delbert Demello
2. Wayne McCay
3. Rick Pass
HM. Harold Brown

Hooded Merganser
1. Wayne Lawson
2. John Wood
3. John Wood
HM. Paul Dibranou

Red-breasted Merganser
1. Rick Pass
2. Harold Brown

Scaup
1. Robert Hanger
2. Linda Gawel

All Other
1. Robert Strachan

Geese, Swan, and Confidence
1. Michael Jackson
2. John Wood

Grebe
1. Michael Jackson
2. John Wood

Decorative Life-size Wildfowl
1. Leonel Gonzales
2. Leonel Gonzales
3. Leonel Gonzales

Waterfowl
1. John Wood
2. John Drewery
3. Scott Lebakken
HM. Augustus Berkeley
HM. Jack Schevel

Shorebirds and Wading Birds
1. David Farrow
2. Raymond Yoast
3. Ralph Bertrand

Seabirds
1. Mark Gizzi
2. Ronald Rosciszewski

Upland Game Birds
1. Michael Jackson

Birds of Prey
1. Linda Gawel
2. Leonel Gonzales
3. Michael Jackson
HM. Carroll Walter
HM. Rob Monkhouse
HM. Dave Paul

Songbirds A
1. Leonel Gonzales
2. Leonel Gonzales
3. Cherylle Vitelli
HM. Joann Burrows
HM. Gloria Liedlich

Songbirds B
1. Linda Gawel
2. Raymond Yoast
3. Dave Paul
HM. Gregorio Celia
HM. Kimberly Rhault

Non-passerine Land Birds
1. Leonel Gonzales
2. Patrick Parrish
3. Gregorio Celia
HM. John Graf
HM. Dave Paul

Decorative Miniature Wildfowl
1. Ralph Bertrand
2. Dave Paul
3. Alan Gabris

Waterfowl
1. Jack Schevel
2. Jack Schnekenburge
3. Ronald Richards
HM. James Galvin

Shorebirds and Wading Birds
1. Alan Gabris
2. Carl Tosi
3. Alan Gabris
HM. Ronald Richards
HM. Charles Ritch
HM. Brenda Scheidler
HM. Ronald Richards
HM. Ronald Richards
HM. Nicholas Gabris

Seabirds
1. Dave Paul
2. Bob Solomon

Birds of Prey
1. Ralph Bertrand
2. Alan Gabris
3. Akinori Okamoto
HM. Charles Skinas
HM. David Findley

Songbirds A
1. Paul Wildisan

Non-passerine Land Birds
1. Judy Read
2. Charles Ritch

Interpretive Wood Sculpture
1. Mark Gizzi
2. Roger Clark
3. Peter Johnson
HM. Richard Marsh
HM. Rick Pass

Bench
1. Micheline Berndt
2. Jay Bundick
3. Peter Johnson

Waterfowl
1. Peter Johnson
2. Jack Kelly
3. John Gratwick
HM. Harold Brown

Shorebirds
1. Daniel Conway
2. Jack Schevel
3. Tom Huntington
HM. Edwin Hind
HM. Alois Guelta
HM. Bob Waltersdorff

Songbirds
1. Debbie Crawford
2. Frank Murray
3. Debbie Crawford
HM. Rick Pass

All Other
1. Micheline Berndt
2. Jay Bundick
3. Andrew Holmes
HM. Peggy Wroten

Feathers Division
1. Thomas Horn
2. Thomas Horn
3. Jeff Rechin

Palm Frond Division
1. Daniel Montano
2. Daniel Montano
3. Tom Christie

LEM AND STEVE WARD
COMPETITION

Contemporary Decoy
1. Vincent Ciola
2. Vincent Ciola
3. Robin Oliver

Marsh Ducks
1. Vincent Ciola
2. Robin Oliver
3. Andrew White

Black Duck
1. Pat Bearden
2. Clarence McKenney
3. Edward Braun, Jr.

Blue-winged Teal
1. Jim Higgins
2. Edward Braun, Jr.
3. Vern Jones

Gadwall
1. Vincent Ciola

Green-winged Teal
1. Ross Smoker
2. Donald Combs
3. Clarence McKenney

Mallard
1. Robin Oliver
2. John Hoover
3. Donald Combs

Northern Pintail
1. Alan Humes
2. Paul Bartlett
3. Donald McHugh

Shoveler
1. Andrew White
2. Wade Johnson
3. Steven Cogar

Wigeon
1. Vincent Ciola
2. Wade Johnson

Wood Duck
1. Robin Oliver
2. Jim Higgins
3. Wil Iturrino

Diving Ducks
1. John Day
2. Gary Shropshire
3. Vincent Ciola

Bufflehead
1. John Day
2. James Galvin

Canvasback
1. Kinny Rice
2. Bruce Mifflin
3. Robert Jones

Common Merganser
1. Ross Smoker
2. Ross Smoker
3. Jason Chuley

Eider
1. Philip Bailey

Goldeneye
1. Charles Belote

Long-tailed Duck
1. Curtis Constance
2. Ross Smoker
3. Edward Clark, Jr.

Red-breasted Merganser
1. Peter Johnson

Redhead
1. Bruce DiVaccaro
2. George Mechelse
3. Pat Bearden

Ring-necked Duck
1. Gary Shropshire
2. Steven Cogar
3. Robin Oliver

Ruddy Duck
1. Pat Bearden
2. Wade Johnson

Scaup
1. Vincent Ciola
2. Vincent Ciola
3. Donald Combs

Scoter
1. Michael Frechette

Geese, Swans, and Confidence
1. Vincent Ciola
2. Ivie Elliot
3. Robin Oliver

Brant
1. Robin Oliver
2. Vern Jones

Coot
1. Mark Fontenot
2. Bob Hand, Jr.
3. Edward Braun, Jr.

Geese
1. Vincent Ciola
2. Ivie Elliot
3. Wade Johnson

Grebe
1. Ross Smoker

Confidence and All Other
1. Ross Smoker
2. Michael Morgart

Gunning Pair
1. Chris Martin
2. Steven Cogar
3. Scott Green

Marsh Ducks
1. Chris Martin
2. Steve Hammond
3. Eugene Merritt

Black Duck
1. Eugene Merritt
2. Mali Vujanic
3. Scott Green
HM. Wil Iturrino
HM. Bruce Munro

Blue-winged Teal
1. Richard Zasimowich
2. Bruce Munro

Green-winged Teal
1. George Williams
2. E.J. Felarise
3. Bruce Munro

Mallard
1. Ronald Clements
2. Robin Oliver
3. Jim Higgins
HM. Jesse Downey

Northern Pintail
1. Eugene Merritt
2. Steve Hammond
3. George Williams

Shoveler
1. Chris Martin
2. Edward Braun, Jr.

Wigeon
1. Steven Cogar
2. Vern Jones

Wood Duck
1. David Farrow
2. Edward Braun, Jr.
3. Skip Couvillion
HM. Richard Zasimowich

Diving Ducks
1. Brian Moyse
2. Brian Moyse
3. Scott Green

Bufflehead
1. Brian Moyse
2. Robert Umphlett
3. Michael Morgart
HM. Bruce Munro
HM. Edward Clark, Jr.

Canvasback
1. Tom Rowe
2. Jeffrey Galat
3. Edward Braun, Jr.
HM. Steve Hammond
HM. Andrew Farrow
HM. Jesse Downey

Common Merganser
1. Robin Oliver

Goldeneye
1. Brian Moyse
2. Mark Kilmister

Hooded Merganser
1. John Day
2. Brian Moyse
3. Robert Umphlett

Long-tailed Duck
1. Pat Bearden
2. Ronnie Young

Red-breasted Merganser
1. Richard Clark
2. Eugene Merritt
3. Bruce Munro
HM. George Williams

Redhead
1. Eugene Merritt
2. Steve Hammond
3. Tom Rowe

Ring-necked Duck
1. Robin Oliver

Ruddy Duck
1. Scott Green

Scaup
1. John Day
2. Tom Rowe
3. John McElfresh
HM. Bruce Munro

Scoter
1. Peter Johnson
2. Bruce Munro

Geese, Swans, and Confidence
1. Steven Cogar
2. Scott Green
3. Brian Moyse

Brant
1. George Williams
2. Russell Fish

Coot
1. William Hinton

Geese
1. Steven Cogar
2. Robin Oliver
3. Bruce Munro

Grebe
1. Donald Dunlap

Confidence and All Others
1. Scott Green

Contemporary Decoy— Champion
1. Pat Godin
2. Tom Christie
3. Jon Jones

Marsh Ducks
1. Tom Christie
2. Jon Jones
3. Jon Jones

Diving Ducks
1. Pat Godin
2. Dick Rhode
3. Jon Jones

Geese, Swan, and Confidence
1. Walter Gaskill
2. David Ricci

Gunning Pair Champion
1. Luke Costilow
2. Luke Costilow
3. Walter Gaskill

Marsh Ducks
1. Luke Costilow
2. Michael Braun
3. Walter Gaskill

Diving Ducks
1. Luke Costilow
2. Walter Gaskill
3. Clint Chase

Geese, Swans, and Confidence
1. Andrew White
2. Raymond Thompson

Contemporary Antique
1. Mike Amaral
2. William Belote
3. Rich Moretz

Marsh Ducks, Pristine
1. Janet Baraby
2. E.J. Felarise
3. Denis Hruza

Marsh Ducks, Worn
1. Mike Amaral
2. Kenneth Hussey
3. Matt Burton
HM. John Novak
HM. Ray Whetzel
HM. Kathleen Webster

Diving Ducks, Pristine
1. Rich Moretz
2. Rich Moretz
3. Rich Moretz

Diving Ducks, Worn
1. William Belote
2. William Belote
3. Mike Amaral
HM. Bruce Eppard
HM. William Belote
HM. Bruce Eppard
HM. Bruce Eppard

Geese, Swans, and Confidence, Pristine
1. Rich Moretz

Geese, Swans, and Confidence, Worn
1. Mike Amaral
2. Bruce Eppard
3. Yves Laurent
HM. Peter Egan
HM. Marty Linton

Shorebirds, Pristine
1. Matt Burton
2. Marty Linton
3. Matt Burton
HM. Ray Whetzel
HM. Ray Whetzel
HM. Ray Whetzel
HM. Donald Dunlap

Shorebirds, Worn
1. William Belote
2. William Belote
3. Mary Linton
HM. Matt Burton

All Other, Pristine
1. Yves Laurent

All Others, Worn
1. William Belote
2. Charlotte Dutton
3. William Kennedy

Shorebird Decoy
1. Bruce DiVaccaro
2. Walter Gaskill
3. Gary De Cew

Avocet, Oystercatcher, Stilt
1. Bruce DiVaccaro
2. Gary De Cew
3. Donald Dunlap
HM. Larry Reader

Curlew, Whimbrel, Godwits
1. Richard Belote

Plovers
1. Ray Whetzel
2. Mark Stewart
3. Larry Reader
HM. Ross Smoker

Ward

Yellowlegs, Red Shank, Green Shank, Solitary Sandpiper
1. Ray Whetzel
2. Michael Morgart
3. Ray Whetzel
HM. Russell Fish

Peep
1. William Beese
2. Larry Reader
3. Larry Reader
HM. Michael Morgart

Turnstone, Dowitchers, Knots
1. Donald Dunlap
2. Ray Whetzel

Bench
1. Ivie Elliot
2. Chris Pusey
3. Bruce Eppard

Waterfowl
1. Chris Pusey
2. Bruce Eppard
3. John Novak
HM. Bob Waltersdorff
HM. Franklin Knight
HM. James Sandison
HM. Wil Iturrino

Shorebirds
1. John Elliot
2. Darrel Wilt
3. Kathleen Webster

Songbirds
1. Ivie Elliott

All Other
1. Ruth Carroll

Decorative Smoothie Waterfowl
1. Joe Tamborra
2. Georges Vincelli
3. Georges Vincelli

Marsh Ducks
1. Georges Vincelli
2. Jeff Moore
3. Robert Nelson

Blue-winged Teal
1. Robert Nelson
2. Robert Nelson
3. William Bailey
HM. Gene Hebert

Gadwall
1. Steve Reiner

Green-winged Teal
1. Jeff Moore
2. Rob Foster
3. Alan Thomas

Mallard
1. Johnny Gasbarrino

Wood Duck
1. Georges Vincelli
2. Alan Thomas
3. Robert Nelson

Diving Ducks
1. Joe Tamborra
2. Joe Tamborra
3. William Bailey

Bufflehead
1. Richmond Cyr

Goldeneye
1. Robert Blain

Hooded Merganser
1. Georges Vincelli

Long-tailed Duck
1. Brooke Bailey

Red-breasted Merganser
1. John Gratwick

Redhead
1. William Bailey

Ring-necked Duck
1. Richmond Cyr

Scoter
1. Joe Tamborra
2. Robert Blain
3. Pat Bearden

All Others
1. Joe Tamborra

Geese, Swan, and Confidence
1. Joe Tamborra
2. Georges Vincelli
3. Alan Thomas

Geese
1. Alan Thomas
2. Gene Hebert

Grebe
1. Joe Tamborra
2. Robert Blain
3. Robert Jancewicz

Confidence and All Others
1. Georges Vincelli
2. Evelyn St. Georges

Decorative Smoothie Shorebirds and Wading Birds
1. Peter Palumbo
2. Peter Palumbo
3. Bruce DiVaccaro

Avocet, Oystercatcher, Stilt
1. Thomas Stewart
2. Justin Zacek
3. Jay Bundick

Curlew, Whimbrel, Godwits
1. Bruce DiVaccaro
2. Thomas Stewart

Dowtichers, Knots, Dunlins
1. Gary De Cew
2. Jim Brace
3. Larry Reader

Phalaropes, Woodcock, Snipe
1. Peter Palumbo
2. Andrew White

Plovers
1. Larry Reader

Small Sandpipers
1. Peter Palumbo
2. Thomas Stewart
3. Larry Reader
HM. Steven Durkee

Large Sandpipers, Turnstone
1. Robert Kroese
2. Jay Bundick
3. Philip Roets

Egrets, Heron
1. Tom Baldwin

All Other Waders and Shorebirds
1. Ivie Elliot

Champagne Waterfowl
1. Peter Johnson
2. Andrew White
3. Richard George

Marsh Ducks
1. Andrew White
2. Richard George
3. Richard George
HM. Kimberly Rhault

Diving Ducks
1. Richard George
2. Patrick Chaumard
3. Don Gabelhouse
HM. Richard George

Geese, Swans, and Confidence
1. Patrick Chaumard
2. Vern Jones
3. Don Gabelhouse

Pelagic and Coastal Seabirds
1. Peter Johnson
2. Gary Stenger
3. Kimberly Rhault

Champagne Waterfowl— Champion
1. Theodore Smith
2. Al Fulford
3. Al Fulford

Marsh Ducks
1. Al Fulford
2. David Harris
3. Russ Clark

Diving Ducks
1. Al Fulford
2. David Harris
3. Russ Clark

Geese, Swans, and Confidence
1. Theodore Smith
2. Russ Clark

Pelagic and Coastal Seabirds
1. Russ Clark
2. Theodore Smith

Decorative Smoothie Waterfowl—Champion
1. Pat Godin
2. Pat Godin
3. Pat Godin

Marsh Ducks
1. Pat Godin
2. Pat Godin
3. Pat Godin

Diving Ducks
1. Ken Stuparyk
2. Jim Brace
3. John Elliot

Geese, Swans, and Confidence
1. Theodore Smith
2. Theodore Smith

A. DANNER FRAZER YOUTH COMPETITION

Decorative Wildfowl (YD2)
1. Jonathan Irons
2. Jonathan Irons
3. Hudson Kinslow
HM. Jordan Thompson
HM. Hudson Kinslow

Decorative Wildfowl (YD3)
1. Kage Guge
2. Worth Kinslow
3. Sophie Clark
HM. Skylar Guge
HM. Worth Kinslow
HM. Harrison Clark

Gunning Decoy (YD2)
1. Donovan Shockley
2. Reed Ford
3. Grayson Russell
HM. Jonathan Russell

Diving Ducks
1. Donovan Shockley
2. Reed Ford
3. Grayson Russell
HM. Jonathan Russell

Silhouette (YS1)
1. Dana Kleman
2. Olivia Hernandes

Silhouette (YS2)
1. Dannie Montano
2. Laura Dutton
3. Adele Blain
HM. Samantha Whaples
HM. Rylan Bedard
HM. Claire Hansen
HM. Layla Neven

Silhouette (YS3)
1. Julian Montano
2. Noah Moretz
3. Ethan Falkinburg
HM. Cooper Paterson
HM. Elsa Blain
HM. Alice Blain
HM. Harrison Schlabach

WILDLIFE SCULPTURE OTHER THAN WOOD
1. David Turner
2. Daniel Burgette
3. David Turner

MEMORIAL AWARDS

Dr. John P. Trabuchi Memorial Award—Best Intermediate Diver
1. Bruce Mifflin

William Schultz Memorial Award—Intermediate Decorative Life-size Wildfowl, Best in Waterfowl
1. Jeannine Audet

Richard "Dick" LeMaster Memorial—Intermediate Decorative Life-size Floating Waterfowl, Best Mallard Hen
1. Dan Meloche

Mike Wavercak Memorial Award—Intermediate Decorative Life-size Floating Waterfowl, Best in Species, Bufflehead
1. Richard Clark

Robert "Bob" Guge Memorial Award, Novice Decorative Life-size Wildfowl, Best Songbird
1. Leonel Gonzales

PEOPLE'S CHOICE AWARD
1. Andrew Tunikov
2. Gary Eigenberger
3. Daniel Montano